The *Malmariée* in the Thirteenth-Century Motet

This monograph offers a comprehensive study of the topos of the *malmariée* or the unhappily married woman within the thirteenth-century motet repertory, a vocal genre characterized by several different texts sounding simultaneously over a foundational Latin chant. Part I examines the *malmariée* motets from three vantage points: (1) in light of contemporaneous canonist views on marriage; (2) to what degree the French *malmariée* texts in the upper voices treat the messages inherent in the underlying Latin chant through parody and/or allegory; and (3) interactions among upper-voice texts that invite additional interpretations focused on gender issues.

Part II investigates the transmission profile of the motets, as well as of their refrains, revealing not only intertextual refrain usage between the motets and other genres, but also a significant number of shared refrains between *malmariée* motets and other motets. Part II furthermore offers insights on the chronology of composition within a given intertextual refrain nexus, and examines how a refrain's meaning can change in a new context. Finally, based on the transmission profile, Part II argues for a lively interest in the topos in the 1270s and 1280s, both through composition of new motets and compilation of earlier ones, with Paris and Arras playing a prominent role.

Dolores Pesce is Avis Blewett Professor of Music at Washington University in St. Louis, specializing in music of the Middle Ages and the late nineteenth century. Her books include *The Affinities and Medieval Transposition*; *Hearing the Motet: Essays on the Motet of the Middle Ages and Renaissance*; *Guido d'Arezzo's Regule rithmice, Prologus in antiphonarium, and Epistola ad Michahelem: A Critical Text and Translation*; and *Liszt's Final Decade*.

Royal Musical Association Monographs
Series Editor: Simon P. Keefe

This series was originally supported by funds made available to the Royal Musical Association from the estate of Thurston Dart, former King Edward Professor of Music at the University of London. The editorial board is the Publications Committee of the Association.

No. 35 **Felice Giardini and Professional Music Culture in Mid-Eighteenth-Century London**
Cheryll Duncan

No. 36 **Disinformation in Mass Media: Gluck, Piccinni and the Journal de Paris**
Beverly Jerold

No. 37 **Music Theory in Late Medieval Avignon: Magister Johannes Pipardi**
Karen M. Cook

No. 38 **Gregorio Ballabene's Forty-eight-part Mass for Twelve Choirs (1772)**
Florian Bassani

No. 39 **Authorship and Identity in Late Thirteenth-Century Motets**
Catherine A. Bradely

No. 40 **The *Malmariée* in the Thirteenth-Century Motet**
Dolores Pesce

For more information about this series, please visit: www.routledge.com/music/series/RMA

The *Malmariée* in the Thirteenth-Century Motet

Dolores Pesce

LONDON AND NEW YORK

First published 2023
by Routledge
4 Park Square, Milton Park, Abingdon, Oxon OX14 4RN

and by Routledge
605 Third Avenue, New York, NY 10158

Routledge is an imprint of the Taylor & Francis Group, an informa business

© 2023 Dolores Pesce

The right of Dolores Pesce to be identified as author of this work has been asserted in accordance with sections 77 and 78 of the Copyright, Designs and Patents Act 1988.

All rights reserved. No part of this book may be reprinted or reproduced or utilised in any form or by any electronic, mechanical, or other means, now known or hereafter invented, including photocopying and recording, or in any information storage or retrieval system, without permission in writing from the publishers.

Trademark notice: Product or corporate names may be trademarks or registered trademarks, and are used only for identification and explanation without intent to infringe.

British Library Cataloguing-in-Publication Data
A catalogue record for this book is available from the British Library

ISBN: 978-1-032-37120-7 (hbk)
ISBN: 978-1-032-37121-4 (pbk)
ISBN: 978-1-003-33540-5 (ebk)

DOI: 10.4324/9781003335405

Typeset in Times New Roman
by codeMantra

Contents

List of Music Examples	vii
List of Manuscripts	ix
List of Abbreviations	xiii
Manuscripts xiii	
Other Abbreviations xv	
Acknowledgments	xvii
Introduction	1
Marriage: Mutual Consent and Marital Debt 2	
Portrayals of Marriage in Literature and Song 4	

PART I
***Malmariée* Motets in Relationship to Their Tenors**   15

1	Paschal Season Liturgy	19
2	Assumption Liturgy	28
3	Other Liturgical Tenors	42
4	French Tenors and French Text Only	54

PART II
***Malmariée* Motet Refrains within an Intertextual Nexus**   61

5	Motet Refrains Shared with Other Genres	63
	With a Song and a Romance or Narrative Poem 63	
	With One or More Songs 77	
	With a Narrative Poem 82	
	Concluding Remarks 84	

6	Motet Refrains Shared with Other Motets	87
	Mo 6, 233 87	
	Mo 5, 148 91	
	Mo 2, 23 and Mo 5, 142 104	
	Mo 2, 30 111	
	Conclusion	114
	Contents 114	
	Transmission and Intertextuality 117	

Appendix A: Tables 1–7	127
Appendix B: Texts and Translations of Motets 60, 62, 67, and 84 from MS N(mo)	143
Bibliography	145
Index of Compositions	155
General Index	157

List of Music Examples

1	Transmission of refrain vdB 1531 melody	74
2	Transmission of refrain vdB 1856 melody	78
3	Transmission of refrain vdB 1691 melody	90
4	Scheme of refrain entrances for **Mo** 5, 148	92
5	Transmission of refrain vdB 532 melody	94
6	Transmission of refrain vdB 750 melody	99
7	Transmission of refrain vdB 1781 melody	101
8	Refrain vdB 750 and tenor *PORTARE*: hypothetical and notated pitch in **Mo** 5, 148	103
9	Transmission of refrain vdB 587 melody in **Mo** 2, 23 and **Mo** 5, 142	106
10	Second half of refrain vdB 587 in **Mo** 2, 23 versus in **Mo** 5, 142 over tenor *PORTARE*	107
11	Transmission of refrain vdB 900 in **Mo** 2, 23 and **Mo** 5, 142	108
12	Transmission of refrain vdB 664 in **Mo** 2, 23 and **Mo** 5, 106	109

List of Manuscripts

This list uses conventional sigla for manuscripts within a given genre. Some manuscripts are listed in more than one section because they transmit more than one genre. Because the sources for each genre were catalogued independently of one another, a given manuscript may appear with a different siglum according to the source type (e.g. motet source N = trouvère source T); these instances are cross-referenced.

Motet Sources

ArsB	Paris, Bibliothèque de l'Arsenal, 3517–18
Ba	Bamberg, Staatsbibliothek, Lit. 115 (formerly Ed.IV.6)
Bes	Besançon, Bibliothèque municipale, I, 716
Cl	Paris, Bibliothèque nationale de France, nouv.acq. fr. 13521, "La Clayette"
Douce 308	Oxford, Bodlein Library, Douce 308
F	Florence, Biblioteca Medicea Laurenziana, Plut. 29.1
Hu	Burgos, Monasterio de la Huelgas, 11 (formerly IX)
LoV	London, British Library, Cotton Vespasian A xviii
Mo	Montpellier, Bibliothèque interuniversitaire, Section de médecine, H. 196
N	Paris, Bibliothèque nationale de France, fr.12651, "Noailles chansonnier" (T in chanson sources)
R	Paris, Bibliothèque nationale de France, fr. 844, "Manuscrit du Roi" (M in chanson sources)
StV	Paris, Bibliothèque nationale de France, lat. 15139, "St Victor"
Tu	Turin, Biblioteca reale, varia 42
Vat. 1543	Vatican City, Biblioteca Apostolica Vaticana, Reg. lat. 1543
W2	Wolfenbüttel, Herzog August Bibliothek, Cod. Guelf. 1099 Helmst. (Heinemann no. 1206)

x List of Manuscripts

Chanson Sources (trouvère, unless otherwise noted)

C	Bern, Burgerbibliothek 389
K	Paris, Bibliothèque de l'Arsenal, 5198
M	Paris, Bibliothèque nationale de France, fr.844, "Manuscrit du Roi" (R in motet sources)
N	Paris, Bibliothèque nationale de France, fr.845
P	Paris, Bibliothèque nationale de France, fr.847
R	Paris, Bibliothèque nationale de France, fr. 1591
T	Paris, Bibliothèque nationale de France, fr.12651, "Noailles chansonnier" (N in motet sources)
U	Paris, Bibliothèque nationale de France, fr. 20050
V	Paris, Bibliothèque nationale de France, fr. 24406
W	Paris, Bibliothèque nationale de France, fr. 25566, "Adam de la Halle manuscript"
X	Paris, Bibliothèque nationale de France, n.a. fr.1050
Z	Siena, Biblioteca Comunale degli Intronati, Sc H.X.36
a	Vatican City, Biblioteca Apostolica Vaticana, Reg. lat. 1490
k	Paris, Bibliothèque nationale de France, fr. 12786
Mod. R.4.4	Modena, Biblioteca Estense, R.4.4
R	Paris, Bibliotheque nationale de France, fr. 22543 (troubadour)

Sources for Romances, Narrative Poems, and Treatises

Roman de la Violette
Paris, Bibliothèque nationale de France, fr. 1374
Paris, Bibliothèque nationale de France, fr. 1553
St. Petersburg, National Library of Russia, fr. 4° v. XIV 3
New York, Pierpont Morgan Library, M. 36

Renart le Nouvel
Paris, Bibliothèque nationale de France, fr. 1593
Paris, Bibliothèque nationale de France, fr. 25566 (W in chanson sources)
Paris, Bibliothèque nationale de France, fr. 372
Paris, Bibliothèque nationale de France, fr. 1581

Court d'amours
Paris, Bibliothèque nationale de France, n.a. fr. 1731

List of Manuscripts   xi

L'art d'amours
Paris, Bibliothèque nationale de France, fr. 881
Paris, Bibliothèque de l'Arsenal, 2741
Modena, Biblioteca Estense, g.G.3.20 (=Campori 42)
Brussels, Bibliothèque royale, 10988

Court de paradis
Paris, Bibliothèque nationale de France, fr. 837
Paris, Bibliothèque nationale de France, fr. 25532
Paris, Bibliothèque nationale de France, fr. 1802

Roman de Fauvel
Paris, Bibliothèque nationale de France, fr. 146

Quinque incitamenta ad Deum amandum ardenter
Vatican City, Biblioteca Apostolica Vaticana, Reg. lat. 71
Troyes, Bibliothèque municipal, 1890
Brussels, Bibliothèque royale, 2475–81

Abbreviations

Manuscripts

Because sigla N and R are used independently in cataloguing motet, trouvère, and troubadour sources, the source type for each of their usages is indicated below by (mo), (trv), or (trb). A reader may consult the List of Manuscripts to determine the source type for all other manuscripts. Cross-references are also explained there.

a	Vatican City, Biblioteca Apostolica Vaticana, Reg. lat. 1490
ArsB	Paris, Bibliothèque de l'Arsenal, 3517–18
Ba	Bamberg, Staatsbibliothek, Lit. 115 (formerly Ed.IV.6)
Bes	Besançon, Bibliothèque municipale, I, 716
C	Bern, Burgerbibliothek, 389
Cl	Paris, BnF, n. a. fr. 13521
Douce 308	Oxford, Bodleian Library, Douce 308
F	Florence, Biblioteca Medicea Laurenziana, Plut. 29.1
Hu	Burgos, Monasterio de las Huelgas, 11 (formerly IX)
k	Paris, BnF, fr. 12786
K	Paris, Bibliothèque de l'Arsenal 5198
KBR 10988	Brussels, Bibliothèque royale, 10988
KBR 2475–81	Brussels, Bibliothèque royale, 2475–81
LoV	London, British Library, Cotton Vespasian A xviii
M	Paris, BnF, fr. 844 = R(mo)
Mo	Montpellier, Bibliothèque interuniversitaire, Section de médecine, H. 196
Mod. g.G.3.20	Modena, Biblioteca Estense, g.G.3.20 (= Campori 42)
Mod. R.4.4	Modena, Biblioteca Estense, R.4.4

xiv *Abbreviations*

N(mo)	Paris, BnF, fr. 12651 = T
N(trv)	Paris, BnF, fr. 845
NY M. 36	New York, Morgan Library, M. 36
P	Paris, BnF, fr. 847
Pa 146	Paris, BnF, fr. 146
Pa 372	Paris, BnF, fr. 372
Pa 837	Paris, BnF, fr. 837
Pa 881	Paris, Bnf, fr. 881
Pa 1374	Paris, BnF, fr. 1374
Pa 1553	Paris, BnF, fr. 1553
Pa 1581	Paris, BnF, fr. 1581
Pa 1593	Paris, BnF, fr. 1593
Pa 1731	Paris, Bnf, n. a. fr. 1731
Pa 1802	Paris, BnF, fr. 1802
Pa 2741	Paris, Bibliothèque de l'Arsenal, 2741
Pa 25532	Paris, BnF, fr. 25532
Pa 25566	Paris, BnF, fr. 25566 = W
R(mo)	Paris, BnF, fr. 844 = M
R(trb)	Paris, BnF, fr. 22543
R(trv)	Paris, BnF, fr. 1591
SP 4° v. XIV 3	St. Petersburg, National Library of Russia, fr. 4° v. XIV 3
StV	Paris, BnF, lat. 15139
T	Paris, BnF, fr.12651 = N(mo)
Tr 1890	Troyes, Bibliothèque municipale, 1890
Tu	Turin, Biblioteca reale, varia 42
U	Paris, BnF, fr. 20050
V	Paris, BnF, fr. 24406
Vat. 71	Vatican City, Biblioteca Apostolica Vaticana, Reg. lat. 71
Vat. 1543	Vatican City, Biblioteca Apostolica Vaticana, Reg. lat. 1543
W	Paris, BnF, fr. 25566
W2	Wolfenbüttel, Herzog August Bibliothek, Cod. Guelf. 1099 Helmst. (Heinemann no. 1206)
X	Paris, BnF, n. a. fr. 1050
Z	Siena, Biblioteca Comunale degli Intronati, Sc H.X.36

Other Abbreviations

BnF	Paris, Bibliothèque nationale de France
EM	Hans Tischler, ed., *The Earliest Motets (to circa 1270): A Complete Comparative Edition* (New Haven, CT: Yale University Press, 1982)
Grove	*Grove Music Online*, https://www.oxfordmusiconline.com/grovemusic
Ludwig	Friedrich Ludwig, *Repertorium organorum recentioris et motetorum vetustissimi stili*, ed. Luther A. Dittmer, 2 vols. in 3 (New York: Institute of Mediaeval Music, 1961–78 [1910])
Gennrich	Friedrich Gennrich, *Bibliographie der ältesten französischen und lateinischen Motetten*, Summa musicae Medii Aevi 2 (Darmstadt: Friedrich Gennrich, 1957)
Saltzstein, *Adam*	Jennifer Saltzstein, ed., *Musical Culture in the World of Adam de la Halle* (Leiden and Boston, MA: Brill, 2019)
RISM	Répertoire International des Sources Musicales
vdB	Nico H. J. van den Boogaard, *Rondeaux et refrains du XIIe siècle au début du XIVe* (Paris: Klincksieck, 1969)

Acknowledgments

I extend my heartfelt thanks to Catherine Bradley and Anne Ibos-Augé for their generous input and feedback during the writing of this book. I am grateful to Simon Keefe, series editor of Royal Musical Association Monographs, who stewarded the book through the review process, to Heidi Bishop at Routledge who oversaw its publication, to Bonnie Blackburn for copyediting the volume, and to Zach Watkins for preparing its music examples.

Introduction

The unhappily married woman or *malmariée* is a well-known topos within the lyric type known as *chanson de femme*, which features a woman's voice in some or all of its lines, her voice constituting the lyric subject ("I") of the song.[1] Whereas many subcategories of the *chanson de femme* convey a mournful tone related to the woman's separation from the man she loves (e.g. the *chanson d'ami* and *auba*), the *chanson de malmariée* seems to be characterized most strongly by a woman's resistance to the constraints of a loveless marriage, most often voiced in a monologue. She may revel in her affair with an already acquired lover or speculate about finding one. Thus, these songs signify more than a complaint about a woman's unhappy marital reality: they also bring to light her defiant response, whether fantasized or real.[2]

Despite scholarly familiarity with the *malmariée* topos, there has been no comprehensive study of it within the thirteenth-century motet repertory.[3] This study fills in the gap by examining the eighteen extant examples, all French-texted, transmitted in manuscripts that date from the mid-thirteenth to the early fourteenth century. This polyphonic genre offers an opportunity for interaction of two (and possibly three) French upper-voice texts with one another and with a pre-existing tenor chant fragment, whose liturgical meanings are known to the

1 See *Songs of the Women Trouvères*, ed., trans., and intro. by Eglal Doss-Quinby et al. (New Haven, CT: Yale University Press, 2001), 7, which provides an overview of how scholars have defined the *chanson de femme*.
2 Anne L. Klinck states that the *mal mariée* genre "brings us to the boundaries of lament" because the speakers are "less mournful than defiant"; "Singing a Song of Sorrow," in *Laments for the Lost in Medieval Literature*, ed. Jan Tolmie and M. J. Toswell (Turnhout: Brepols, 2010), 115–16.
3 An important contributing study is Anna Kathryn Grau, "Representation and Resistance: Female Vocality in Thirteenth-Century France" (Ph.D. diss., University of Pennsylvania, 2010).

DOI: 10.4324/9781003335405-1

listener. The *malmariée*'s utterances may be interpreted as an allegorical or parodic play on the tenor's text. But they also interact with the rhetoric of the upper-voice text(s), often spoken by a male in the *grand chant courtois* tradition. Elements of the *pastourelle*, signaled by an encounter between its male narrator and an assertive shepherdess, also surface, directly or through intertextual refrain usage. The aural play of male and female voices reveals motet creators' interest in exploring an idea of womanhood as portrayed in contemporary song and narrative. The contrast between the insecure, idealizing male and the confident female can be striking. At the same time, the married women's voices expose an awareness of the very real constraints they faced in medieval society.

Marriage: Mutual Consent and Marital Debt

Around 1100, when the Church sought to remodel social life and counter the imbalance of a patriarchal society, its main strategy was the promotion and sanctification of the institution of marriage.[4] The issues of mutual consent and marital debt lay at the heart of churchmen's discussions about the foundational principles of marriage. In the mid-twelfth century, the two major schools of canonical thought differed in their view of whether consummation was requisite to marriage: the Italian, following Gratian (*Decretum*, ca. 1140), required consummation, and the French, following Peter Lombard (*Sententiae*, 1155–58), did not. But they agreed on the necessity of mutual consent, whereby both individuals agreed to the marriage. Through a decretal in 1180, Pope Alexander III effectively established that mutual consent was the essential ingredient in marriage. Putting this requirement into place reflected the Church's efforts to introduce elements of gender symmetry into the agreement.[5] Later canonists, following Gratian's lead in his *Decretum*, considered that marriage, once consummated, "created

---

4 Georges Duby, "The Matron and the Mis-Married Woman: Perceptions of Marriage in Northern France circa 1100," in *Social Relations and Ideas: Essays in Honour of R. H. Hilton*, ed. T. H. Aston, P. R. Coss, Christopher Dyer, and Joan Thirsk (New York: Cambridge University Press, 1983), 89. For a broader overview of medieval attitudes toward marriage, as well as excerpts from relevant literary sources, see Carolyne Larrington, *Women and Writing in Medieval Europe: A Sourcebook* (London and New York: Routledge, 1995), 7–38.
5 John W. Baldwin, "Consent and the Marital Debt: Five Discourses in Northern France around 1200," in *Consent and Coercion to Sex and Marriage in Ancient and Medieval Societies*, ed. Angeliki E. Laiou (Washington, DC: Dumbarton Oaks, 1993), 258.

a second and discrete set of mutual obligations called the marital debt (*debitum*), whereby married partners were required to respond fully to each other's sexual demands."[6] Again, this concept represented an attempt by the Church to construct a symmetrical balance between the spouses; marital debt could be nullified only by mutual agreement (related to issues of impotence, disease, and religious vocations).[7]

But the Church's attempts to introduce gender symmetry did not go unchallenged. Women continued to be susceptible to the "patrimonial preoccupations" of the aristocratic class, which had made arranged marriages the norm.[8] Within the aristocratic model, women agreed to arranged marriages because they considered them their underlying duty; in some cases, nominal consent might even represent a woman's response to pressure from and fear of her guardian.[9] A woman's consent was further compromised by the introduction of marital debt into the equation. Although the Church intended the concept to place women on equal footing with men, in effect it could place women in the untenable position of having to continue in a loveless marriage and submit to forced sexual relations. The matter of consent was also complicated by physicians' views on the roles of men and women in the reproductive act. Since the eleventh century, physicians subscribed to a two-seed theory whereby both male and female emit seed simultaneously to bring about conception; furthermore, desire must underlie that emission, with both partners being aroused at the same time. Yet this gender symmetry contended with a pronouncement by the same physicians that female desire was greater than that of the male, thereby challenging the reciprocity of the marital debt. At least one *fabliau*, the thirteenth-century *La Dame qui aveine demanoit pour Morel sa provende avoir*, offers a dictum in response to the claimed sexual imbalance caused by the wife's greater desire: "I do not say at her wish but at the will of her husband." In effect, this *fabliau* reveals an outlook that mutual consent should be replaced by the dominance of the

---

6 Ibid., 259.
7 Ibid.; see also Elizabeth M. Makowski, "The Conjugal Debt and Canon Law," *Journal of Medieval History* 3 (1977): 99–114.
8 Baldwin, "Consent and the Marital Debt," 257; in this essay, Baldwin refers to the foundational work on aristocratic marriage by George Duby in *Medieval Marriage: Two Models from Twelfth-Century France*, trans. Elborg Forster (Baltimore, MD and London: The Johns Hopkins University Press, 1978), 83–110.
9 Noël James Menuge, "Female Wards and Marriage in Romance and Law: A Question of Consent," in *Young Medieval Women*, ed. Katherine J. Lewis et al. (New York: St. Martin's Press, 1999), 153–71.

man in order to restore gender equilibrium. It is unclear how widely held this outlook was.[10]

Despite these impediments to gender symmetry, historians allow that some progress was achieved through the canonists' efforts in the twelfth century. Yet the possibility of marital bondage increased when, in the first decade of the thirteenth century, Aristotle's writings became available in Paris. Writers such as David de Dinant in his *Quaternuli* promoted Aristotelian ideas that the female's role in conception is passive and female pleasure unnecessary in order to conceive. Although Church theologians condemned the Aristotelian treatises in 1210 and again in 1215, Paris theologians, most notably Albertus Magnus and Thomas Aquinas, rehabilitated them during the course of the thirteenth century.[11] Accordingly, the physiological basis for gender symmetry, based upon reciprocal contribution and desire, was undermined, leading to further erosion of the gender symmetry intended by the Church's twelfth-century decrees.

Portrayals of Marriage in Literature and Song

Against this historical backdrop, we examine to what degree gender symmetry, particularly in marriage, is portrayed in treatises on love, various literary genres, and in song. Importantly, Ovid's *Ars amatoria* remained the authoritative text on lovemaking in the twelfth century, and in the thirteenth century was made available in a French translation and commentary entitled *L'Art d'amours*.[12] Ovid's views essentially match those of the Church: he explicitly argues for gender symmetry and mutual consent, even offering a technique for achieving

---

10 Baldwin discusses the *fabliau* in "Consent and Marital Debt," 267–68.
11 Ibid., 269–70.
12 In his translation of *L'Art d'amours* (The Art of Love), Garland Library of Medieval Literature, series A, vol. 32 (New York and London: Garland Publishing, Inc., 1987), x, Lawrence B. Blonquist argues that Books I and II were written separately from Book III, with the first two dating from the first third of the century, the third book at least thirty to fifty years later. Blonquist's conclusions seem to be based on the work of Bruno Roy, ed., *L'Art d'amours: Traduction et commentaire de l'Ars amatoria de Ovide* (Leiden: E. J. Brill, 1974), 56–57. Roy specifically mentions that Books I and II were written after 1214–15, but within the first third of the century; and Book III after 1268, but before the century ended.

For a study of the use within the repertory of four refrains derived from this Ovidian text, see Jennifer Saltzstein, "Ovid and the Thirteenth-Century Motet: Quotation, Reinterpretation, and Vernacular Hermeneutics," *Musica disciplina* 58 (2013): 351–72.

simultaneous orgasm.[13] Likewise, *fabliaux* are noteworthy for featuring couples who experience mutual consent and sexual reciprocity. With respect to romances, John Baldwin maintains that their writers "transformed into a prescribed ideal" the concept of gender symmetry that had been promoted by the theologians, physicians, and Ovidians.[14] Most notably, Chrétien de Troyes (fl. ca. 1160–91) created characters in *Eric et Enide* and in *Cligès* who marry not through coercion, but instead prompted by mutual consent, love, and desire. Jean Renart (early thirteenth century) likewise presents in his romances *L'Escoufle* and *Roman de la rose* couples who fall in love and eventually marry, in the latter despite objections related to the partners' different social status.

On the other hand, some writers acknowledge marital bondage, including specific mention of marital debt. Marie de France (fl. 1160–1215) depicts in several of her narrative poems wives unhappily imprisoned in marriage: in both *Yonec* and *Guigemar*, actual imprisonment takes place when an elderly husband physically confines his wife, restricting her freedom to go where she wishes. In both cases, the wife takes a lover, thereby defying her Christian pledge of marital fidelity. Acknowledgment of marital bondage also appears in writings that predate Marie de France. Heloise (b. c. 1100–01?, d. 16 May 1163–64?) wrote in the early twelfth century of coercive marital bonds (*vincula nuptualis, matrimonii foedera*). Andreas Capellanus related in his twelfth-century treatise *De amore* a statement that "love cannot exist between two married people" in the letter that he attributed to Marie, countess of Champagne. She noted that wedded couples are "yoked together, compelled by marriage obligation to submit to their mutual will and in no way able to deny themselves to each other."[15] Thus, this Marie speaks directly of the constraints imposed by the marital debt.

What about the portrayal of marriage in medieval French song? In the troubadour *canso* and trouvère *grand chant courtois*, the unattainable woman to whom the poetry is addressed may be a married woman, based on information we glean from the *vidas* and from the poetic texts themselves.[16] But we are not privy to the woman's reflections.

---

13 Baldwin, "Consent and the Marital Debt," 263, summarizes Ovid's advice in *Ars amatoria*, with reference to E. J. Kenney, ed., *Amores. Medicamina faciei feminaeae. Ars amatoria. Remedia amoris*, new ed. (New York: Oxford University Press, 1994).
14 Baldwin, "Consent and the Marital Debt," 263.
15 Ibid., 265.
16 See S. B. Gaunt, "Marginal Men, Marcabru and Orthodoxy: The Early Troubadours and Adultery," *Medium Ævum* 59 (1990): 55–72; and *Songs of the Women*

The lyrics instead focus on the thoughts and feelings of the man who seeks her favor, in whose voice the poetry unfolds.[17]

As noted at the outset, women do speak in the lyric type known as *chanson de femme*, and married women in particular in the subgenre known as *chanson de malmariée*. *Chansons de femme*, typically anonymous, emanated from northern France at the time of the trouvères. While it has traditionally been assumed that males wrote the *chanson de femme* lyrics, some scholars argue that we should be open to the possibility that women authored some of the anonymous songs.[18] A related issue is the long-lived tendency to categorize *chansons de femme* as revealing a popularizing register (*registre popularisant*) as opposed to the learned or courtly register (*registre aristocratisant*) of the trouvère *grand chant courtois* or the troubadour *canso*, terminology introduced by Pierre Bec in 1969 and repeated again in 1977.[19]

Nonetheless, Bec himself recognized in 1977 that the *chansons de femme* in fact display many traits associated with the courtly register, that is, they partake of what he termed *interférences registrales* (borrowing between registers).[20] Following from Bec's and other scholars' research, we now have a more flexible understanding of registers, allowing that various medieval lyric types did not exist in opposition, but more likely fed off one another.[21] Bec in fact theorized that when the trobairitz adapted the troubadour *cansos* to the female voice, they drew on themes they found in the *chansons de femme*.[22] Which brings us to the argument for a pre-literate tradition of women's songs. Support for

---

Trouvères, 37: "While it is true that adultery is not a mandatory feature of the love relationship described by fin'amors, it is a theme that appears in Old French lyrics."
17 A woman's voice does come through in the *cansos* attributed to female troubadours or *trobaritz*. In these cases, the speaker, rather than being the sought-after woman, seeks love herself.
18 This view is articulated in *Songs of the Women Trouvères*, 11–14.
19 P. Bec, "Quelques réflexions sur la poésie lyrique médiéval: Problèmes et essai de caractérisation," in *Mélanges offerts à Rita Lejeune*, 2 vols. (Gembloux: Ducolot, 1969), 2: 1309–29; and *La Lyrique française au moyen-âge (XIIe–XIIIe siècles): Contribution à une typologie des genres poétiques médiévaux*, 2 vols. (Paris: Picard, 1977–78). Grimbert provides an overview and critique of Bec's theories published from 1969 through 1979 in "Songs by Women and Women's Songs," in *The Court Reconvenes: Courtly Literature across the Disciplines*, ed. Barbara K. Altmann and Carleton W. Carroll (Cambridge: D. S. Brewer, 2003), 117–24.
20 Bec, *La Lyrique française*, 1: 57–119.
21 *Songs of the Women Trouvères*, 8.
22 Ibid., 10–11, summarizing Bec, "'Trobairitz' et chansons de femme: Contribution à la connaissance du lyrisme féminin au moyen âge," *Cahiers de civilisation médiévale* 22 (1979): 235–62.

Introduction 7

such a theory lies in denouncements against indecent women's songs by churchmen already in the fourth century, by the Council of Châlons in 650, and in a capitulary of Charlemagne from 789.[23] The theory of an oral medieval tradition of women's song was fortified by a 1948 discovery by Samuel Stern of what appear to be the oldest surviving secular lyrics in a Romance vernacular, the Mozarabic *kharjas*, composed around 1000, which serve as refrains or final strophes in the lyric genre known as *muwashshaha*. In the *kharjas*, women voice their yearning, following upon their male counterpart's expression of unrequited love in the preceding strophes.[24] Significantly, these surviving *kharjas* attest to an oral vernacular lyric tradition prior to the first compositions of the earliest troubador Guilhem IX, thereby suggesting that the *chanson de femme* existed before and simultaneously with the troubadour *canso*, in a tradition "vigorous enough to influence the poetry of the troubadours and subsequently to compete with it."[25]

With respect to the specific origin of the *chanson de malmariée*, Alfred Jeanroy theorized in 1892 about a pre-literate medieval tradition in which women composed songs, probably in combination with dance, for the *maieroles* or *fêtes de mai*. He claimed that the earliest songs were essentially *chansons de malmariée*, in view of the fact that the *maieroles* "often featured a May Queen who led the dance with her female companions, excluding the *gelos*—the husband and all those who did not love."[26]

The jealous husband and the "other" man who knows how to truly love appear in the *chansons de malmariée* transmitted in the thirteenth century. While many wives in these songs speak directly of their lovers' ability to please them, they also make clear that sleeping with a lover is revenge against a boorish and at times abusive husband, whose treatment of her warrants her complaint. Simply put, the *malmariée*

---

23 *Songs of the Women Trouvères*, 13.
24 Ibid.
25 Ibid. The earliest *muwashshaha* that preserve the *kharjas* in question were composed around 1000, but this genre was introduced in Moslem Spain around 900, "and there is no reason to believe that the Romance songs presumably known by the earliest practitioners of the *muwashshaha* were a novelty at that time." See also Peter Dronke, *The Medieval Lyric*, 3rd ed. (Woodbridge, Suffolk: D. S. Brewer, 1996), 89–90.
26 See *Songs of the Women Trouvères*, 12, which summarizes Alfred Jeanroy's findings in *Les Origines de la poésie lyrique en France au moyen âge* (Paris: Hachette, 1889; 4th ed., Paris: Honoré Champion, 1965), 445, 88–91, and 389–91, and includes this quotation by Gustav Paris in his review of Jeanroy's book in *Journal des Savants* (1892): 416.

speaks defiantly against the bonds of marriage and marital debt, gaining some upper hand, as shown in this rondeau text:

> *Be patient, husband, and may it not irk you,*
> *Tomorrow you will have me and my lover will tonight.*
> *I forbid you to speak one word of it.*
> *Be patient, husband, and do not move.*
> *The night is short, soon you will have me again,*
> *When my lover has had his pleasure.*
> *Be patient, husband, and may it not irk you,*
> *Tomorrow you will have me and my lover will tonight.*[27]

While the wife's address to the husband recognizes her marital debt, it also stipulates that she has agency to put her lover first.

In some lyrics, the *malmariée* may even revel in the prospect of publicly embarrassing her husband, as revealed in the second strophe of this ballette, with repeated ending refrain for its three strophes:

> And if he won't let me be
> Or lead the good life,
> I'll have him called a cuckold [*Je lou ferai cous clameir*]
> For sure.
> *Why does my husband beat me?*
> *Poor wretch!*[28]

The wife implies that she has asked the husband to treat her better and perhaps desist from forced sexual relations. Expecting his non-compliance, she intends to get revenge by having him publicly derided as a cuckold.

Another mention of a cuckold appears in this excerpt from a *chanson avec des refrains* ascribed to the Duchesse de Lorraine, in which the wife speaks to her lover:

> Beloved, if you desire
> The death of the jealous one,
> Even more do I desire it, so help me God,
> A hundred times more than you!
> He is old and besotted,

---

27 Translation from *Songs of the Women Trouvères*, 185–86.
28 Ibid., 154.

Gluttonous as a wolf,
And scrawny and bald,
And he has a cough.
He has so many foul traits,
The perfidious redhead;
The greatest merit he has
Is to be a cuckold. [*Tote le graindre bonteis c'est de ceu k'il est cous.*]
Friend, alas that I was ever born,
When my body is captive because of you
And another has his will;
Rightfully do I complain:
*How can a lady without her lover heal
When love torments her.*[29]

Near the end, reflecting on having to submit to the will of the husband, the wife invokes Job's lament at being born. Immediately before, she revels in knowing that she can cuckold him. In this song as in the last, turning her husband into a cuckold seems to give the unhappily married wife some bit of pleasure (and agency) in a situation where she otherwise feels helpless.

According to Helen Dell, the ultimate helplessness of the unhappily married women in these songs is suggested by both her tone and the songs' formal unfolding. While the first-person utterances directly express anger and frustration, they at times also contain light-hearted, throwaway lines of defiance against the husband and specifically about taking a lover. Dell asks whether such disconnect between message and manner of presentation suggests a mockery of the woman's actual inability to bring about change in her situation. The use of a repeated refrain such as *Why does my husband beat me? Poor wretch!* contributes to this sense of mockery: that she repeats these words at the end each strophe after admitting to her extra-marital dalliances makes her seem ridiculous.[30] Leaving aside for the moment Dell's interpretation that the repeated refrain mocks the unhappily married wife, it is indisputable that no matter how many times she speaks these words, nothing changes in her fundamental state. She remains imprisoned in a bad marriage.

---

29 Ibid., 160.
30 Helen Dell, *Desire by Gender and Genre in Trouvère Song*, Gallica 10 (Woodbridge, Suffolk and Rochester, NY: D. S. Brewster, 2008), ch. 5, particularly 125–28.

Following from Dell's theory, a comment is in order about the reality of a husband beating his wife in medieval society. Various studies by James A. Brundage between 1987 and 2000 document efforts by canonists of the time to establish guidelines as to when husbands were justified in disciplining their wives through physical means, and when discipline became abusive.[31] More recently, in her book *Medieval Violence: Physical Brutality in Northern France 1270–1330*,[32] Hannah Skoda has expanded the study of domestic violence to include evidence from legal prosecution and contemporary popular literature, such as *fabliaux* and miracles tales. Skoda's chapter "Domestic Violence in Paris and Artois" provides evidence that wife-beating was an issue of concern beyond Paris, particularly in Artois and surrounding areas.[33] Her insight is an important backdrop for the present study, which argues that a handful of the thirteenth-century motets that cultivate the *malmariée* topos reveal a strong northern French connection, particularly centered on Artois and neighboring regions.

Lastly, Skoda's arguments can be brought into conversation with Dell's about the mocking tone of the *malmariée* refrain quoted above, *Why does my husband beat me? Poor wretch!* Skoda writes about *fabliaux* and miracle tales that refer to domestic violence:

> Such texts drew on the experience of their diverse audiences to engage them through bawdy laughter with the problems presented by the interpretation of domestic violence; they questioned and undermined even the fluid lines between discipline and abuse established in prescriptive legal and moral discourse. Both abusive husbands and their victims were made into figures of fun for audiences with whom these inconclusive themes would have resonated uncomfortably.[34]

---

31 James A. Brundage, "Domestic Violence in Classical Canon Law," in *Violence in Medieval Society*, ed. Richard W. Kaeuper (Rochester, NY: Boydell Press, 2000), 183–95; *Law, Sex, and Christian Society in Medieval Europe* (Chicago, IL: University of Chicago Press, 1987); and *Medieval Canon Law* (London: Longman, 1995).

32 Hannah Skoda, *Medieval Violence: Physical Brutality in Northern France 1270–1330* (Oxford: Oxford University Press, 2013).

33 Skoda mentions in particular several *jeux partis* (debate poems) from the Puy of thirteenth-century Arras, and a *fabliau*, *La Mégère emasculée* from mid-thirteenth century Picardy. She elucidates actual practice in exacting punishments of husbands for domestic violence, such as when the favor of the corrupt *bailli* was bought in a case in Arras in 1294, resulting in the release of the offending husband. Ibid., 193–231.

34 Ibid., 197.

Skoda thus argues for hearing intentional mockery in popular literature, which agrees with Dell's interpretation of some *malmariée* songs. But Skoda also reads these popular texts as questioning the *status quo*. Does allowing these related possibilities bring us any closer to fathoming the identity of the anonymous authors in these various genres? Although the present study does not grapple in detail with the thorny issue of authorship, it nonetheless acknowledges that woman's song could be written by a woman or a man.[35] Either could question the status quo. A woman author could directly mock the coarse, brutal husband, while a man could intend for listeners to interpret a *malmariée* in an unfavorable manner. As Dell suggests, he might mock the woman by having her repeatedly ask why her husband beats her, as though she is clueless. Might he also signal that the woman's adulterous behavior casts her, rather than her demanding husband, in the role of transgressor? Might a male author express a male fantasy by depicting the *malmariée* as a physical being, always ready for a sexual encounter? And whether the author is a man or woman, the *malmariée*'s openness to having a lover might be read as a female fantasy. The study's textual analyses consider all these possibilities.

Part I examines the entire *malmariée* motet corpus in the thirteenth century to gain insight into the treatment of the topos within a relatively concentrated period of time. It assumes three vantage points: (1) in light of contemporaneous canonist views on marriage; (2) to what degree the *malmariée* texts respond to the underlying liturgical tenor

---

35 See Anne L. Klinck, "The Oldest Folk Poetry? Medieval Woman's Song as 'Popular' Lyric," in *From Arabye to Engelond: Medieval Studies in Honour of Mahmoud Manzalaoui on His 75th Birthday*, ed. A. E. C. Canitz and Gernot R. Wieland (Ottawa: University of Ottawa Press, 1999), 243; and Wendy Pfeffer, "Complaints of Women and Complaints by Women: Can One Tell Them Apart?," in *The Court Reconvenes*, ed. Barbara K. Altmann and Carleton W. Carroll, 125–32. See also the recent study by Brianne Dolce, "'Soit hom u feme': New Evidence for Women Musicians and the Search for the 'Women Trouvères.'" *Revue de Musicologie* 106 (2020): 301–28. Dolce discusses evidence of women's roles as musicians within the Confraternity of Jongleurs and Bourgeois of Arras, as recorded in a manuscript, Paris, BnF, fr. 8541, copied between the early thirteenth and fifteenth centuries. Though the document labels no women as the equivalent of trouvères, Dolce argues for that possibility, extrapolating from the facts that (1) connections between Arras and Dutch-speaking Brabant and Flanders are evident from the Confraternity's membership and historical documentation; (2) the Dutch-speaking Hadewijch (living over 100 km northeast of Arras) wrote Latin lyrics that apparently contrafacted trouvère lyrics, showing a particular familiarity with the Arrageois trouvères; (3) women in Arras funded and joined religious movements such as the one to which Hadewijch belonged and for which she presumably created her lyrics.

messages through parody and/or allegory; and (3) interactions among a motet's upper-voice texts that invite additional interpretations focused on gender issues.

Part II of the study investigates the total transmission profile of the motets, as well as of their refrains, revealing not only intertextual refrain usage between the motets and such genres as chanson, romance, narrative poems, and treatises, but also a significant number of shared refrains between *malmariée* motets and other motets. Accordingly, the evidence of the *malmariée* motets supports a growing recognition by scholars that motet creators included motets among their refrain sources.[36] Part II offers insights on chronology of composition: for a given intertextual refrain nexus, the possible order in which the pieces (including *contrafacta*) were composed can become apparent through a comparative study of music and text. We learn about the varied ways a motet creator could treat a pre-existing refrain in a context of intergeneric play, such as retaining its speaker's gender and its meaning fairly intact, or switching the speaker's gender and the refrain's meaning accordingly. These treatments yield insights into the different ways love was experienced by men and women in the thirteenth century. We also witness motet creators integrating multiple refrains into sophisticated musical and textual creations.

Finally, the total source profile of the *malmariée* corpus suggests that this topos carved out a space in a limited number of motet manuscripts: Montpellier, Bibliothèque interuniversitaire, Section de médecine, H. 1196 (**Mo**) (produced in Paris); Wolfenbüttel, Herzog August Bibliothek, Cod. Guelf. 1099 Helmst. (**W2**) (probably produced in Paris); and several manuscripts from northern France: two of Artesian origin—Paris, Bibliothèque nationale de France, fr. 12615, "Noailles chansonnier," henceforth motet source **N(mo)**, and Paris, Bibliothèque nationale de France, fr. 844, "Manuscrit du Roi," henceforth motet source **R(mo)**, and one from Lorraine, Oxford, Bodleian Library, **Douce 308**.[37] Scholars have previously noted a relationship among **Mo**, **W2**, and **N(mo)**, without specifying the particular path of transmission. Although this study does not settle that question, it pro-

---

36 See Jennifer Saltzstein, "Relocating the Thirteenth-Century Refrain: Intertextuality, Authority and Origins," *Journal of the Royal Musical Association* 135 (2010): 245–79.

37 See Abbreviations for an explanation of how sigla **N** and **R** have been used independently in cataloguing motet, trouvère, and troubadour sources, a confusing situation clarified by adding **(mo)**, **(trv)**, or **(trb)** to indicate the source type in a given instance.

vides some additional tantalizing evidence on this manuscript nexus. Importantly, an analysis of the overall transmission profile suggests that *malmariée* motets were cultivated and compiled most actively in the 1270s and 1280s, with Parisian **Mo** playing a central role. Within that time framework, **Mo** and **N(mo)** reveal a penchant for cultivating in particular new *malmariée* motets on Assumption chants, pitting the earthly, unhappily married woman against Mary, the devoted heavenly Bride of Christ.

Part I
Malmariée Motets in Relationship to Their Tenors

This study considers eighteen motets from the thirteenth century that engage the *malmariée* topos in some way, without imposing a strictly defined category. As noted earlier, Bec observed borrowing among registers in the song repertory; he also commented that the subgroups of the *chanson de femme* exhibit a tendency to adopt and combine features of other subgroups of *chanson de femme*.[1] Following from Bec's observation, Susan M. Johnson includes forty poems as *chansons de malmariée* because they treat the theme, but not to the exclusion of features found in other *chansons de femme*.[2] For instance, she comments on the use of the encounter frame, familiar from the *pastourelle*, in which a male "I" persona who is out riding encounters a shepherdess whom he engages in conversation. In the context of a *malmariée* encounter, the narrator explains how he happened to overhear a married woman's lament, after which the poem presents her voice. In this hybrid context, the narrator does not necessarily converse with the woman as he would in the *pastourelle*. Another hybrid usage occurs when the married woman mentions her husband in passing, but concentrates instead on the positive qualities of her lover, either real or hoped for, thus adopting a feature of the *chanson d'ami*.[3] In the end,

---

1 Bec, *La Lyrique française*, 1: 57–68, 80–81. Bec diagrams the subcategories of the *chanson de femme* on p. 68. On pp. 62–63 he states: "Elle met en scène une jeune fille qui chante sa joi d'avoir un ami qui l'aime ou, plus fréquement, se plaint de n'en avoir point ou que celui-ci l'ait trahie."

2 Susan M. Johnson, "The *Malmariée* Theme in Old French Lyric or What is a *Chanson de Malmariée*?," in *"Chançon legiere a chanter": Essays on Old French Literature in Honor of Samuel N. Rosenberg*, ed. Karen Fresco and Wendy Pfeffer (New York: Summa Publications, Inc., 2007), 133–51, especially 148.

3 See Bec, *La Lyrique française*, 1: 62–63: "Elle met en scène une jeune fille qui chante sa joi d'avoir un ami qui l'aime ou, plus fréquement, se plaint de n'en avoir point ou que celui-ci l'ait trahie."

DOI: 10.4324/9781003335405-2

Johnson includes these hybrid examples in her corpus of forty poems, acknowledging that approximately twenty would qualify "if we insist on the poem dominated by the woman's voice (either in monologue or dialogue or with a brief encounter frame)."[4]

The present study of thirteenth-century motets follows Bec's and Johnson's lead by including in the corpus motets which engage the *malmariée* topos in some way, without necessarily insisting that an example focus on a sole woman's voice. As shown in Appendix A, Table 1, under the column heading "Manner of Presentation," twelve of the eighteen motets present a monologue spoken by a woman (or women).[5]) Although the female speaker is not always identified as married or anticipating marriage, the rhetoric of the text invites this interpretation as one possibility. Three other motets (**Mo 6, 203, Mo 6, 233, Mo 5, 148**) engage in a different manner of presentation by adopting an encounter frame familiar from the *pastourelle*. In their intergeneric play, the opening gambit sets up an expectation that the narrator will encounter a shepherdess, but he instead comes upon a married woman who speaks to herself, to her husband, or to her lover. Another motet (**Mo 2, 23**) begins with an encomium of Love's power before the woman speaks. The remaining two motets are more idiosyncratic in their approach: **Mo 5, 169** includes no utterance by a woman, but the upper-voice texts invoke the image of a jealous, cuckolded husband through a third-person usage. **Mo 7, 276** stands apart, given that its speaker seems to be a married man.

The following analysis examines this corpus of motets, all with French upper-voice texts: six two-voice, eight three-voice, two four-voice, and two single French texts that survive without tenor (see Table 1 summary). This part of the study examines the textual content of these motets, which, like *malmariée* songs, offer reflections on mutual consent and marital debt. Through the juxtaposition of a *malmariée* upper-voice text with a tenor chant fragment that carries spiritual meaning, allegorical and/or parodic readings can result. Furthermore, the *malmariée* text, by interacting with other upper-voice text(s), may invite additional interpretations through the intergeneric play of the *malmariée* topos with the *grand chant courtois* and *pastourelle*

---

4 Johnson, "The *Malmariée* Theme," 148.
5 In one of these cases, **Mo 6, 180**, the voice of the married woman is heard only in the opening refrain, which has been taken from a *chanson de malmariée* and incorporated into a *chanson pieuse*.

Malmariée *Motets in Relationship to Their Tenors* 17

traditions in particular, and, in so doing, shed light on gendered roles in matters of love. The discussion begins by examining the textual content of the thirteen motets with Latin tenors, grouped by their liturgical associations: paschal season, the Assumption, and three not linked to either of those liturgies. A final chapter examines the remaining four motets that survive with a French-texted tenor or as a French text with no tenor; absent a liturgical tenor, these *malmariée* texts can nonetheless be interpreted in view of (1) marital realities in the thirteenth century and (2) their interactions with a motet's other French texts in depictions of love.

Given that Montpellier, Bibliothèque interuniversitaire, Section de médecine, H. 1196 (**Mo**) is the main transmitter of motets that treat the *malmariée* topos, containing fourteen of the total eighteen, the following discussion uses **Mo** numbers for those fourteen, and EM numbers (from Tischler's *The Earliest Motets*) for another three[6]; the remaining motet, **Tu**, f. 16, unavailable in a published edition, is referred to by its siglum. Unless otherwise indicated, texts and translations for the fourteen motets found in **Mo** are derived from Part 4 of *The Montpellier Codex* edition.[7] For the four remaining *malmariée* motets and related versions of all eighteen, the study derives texts and translations from relevant editions, as indicated in footnotes. Table 1 identifies upper-voice text incipits by their Gennrich numbers (with the spellings he established), and tenor incipits by their Ludwig numbers.[8] The text discussion spells upper-voice text incipits as they appear in a particular manuscript source. Text refrains are identified by their van den Boogaard (vdB) numbers throughout; the tables use the refrain spellings van den Boogaard established, while the text spells them as they

---

6 H. Tischler, ed. *The Earliest Motets (to circa 1270): A Complete Comparative Edition* (New Haven, CT: Yale University Press, 1982).

7 The texts and translations derive from *The Montpellier Codex, Part 4: Texts and Translations,* translations by Susan Stakel and Joel C. Relihan, Recent Researches in the Music of the Middle Ages and Early Renaissance, vol. 8 (Madison, WI: A-R Editions, Inc., 1985). Used with permission. www.areditions.com

8 Friedrich Gennrich, *Bibliographie der ältesten französischen und lateinischen Motetten,* Summa musicae Medii Aevi 2 (Darmstadt: Friedrich Gennrich, 1957); Friedrich Ludwig, *Repertorium organorum recentioris et motetorum vetustissimi stili,* ed. Luther A. Dittmer, 2 vols. in 3 (New York: Institute of Mediaeval Music, 1961–78 [1910]).). Any emendations to the Ludwig and Gennrich numbers noted by Hendrik van der Werf in his *Integrated Directory of Organa, Clausulae, and Motets* (Rochester, NY: Hendrik van der Werf, 1989), have been included.

18 Malmariée *Motets in Relationship to Their Tenors*

appear in a particular manuscript source.[9] Music examples are prepared by the author and retain the text spellings of a particular manuscript source.

---

9 For vdB numbers, see Nico H. J. van den Boogaard, *Rondeaux et refrains du XIIe siècle au début du XIVe* (Paris: Klincksieck, 1969). For the most up-to-date information on refrain sources, I have consulted the online catalogue *Refrain* (http://refrain.ac.uk/) prepared by Anne Ibos-Augé. Her catalogue is invaluable because it includes the melody that accompanies a refrain in a given source. See also Hans G. Spanke, *Raynaud's Bibliographie des altfranzösischen Liedes*, Musicologica 1 (Leiden: Brill, 1955).

1 Paschal Season Liturgy

Five motets in this corpus use tenor chant fragments from the paschal season liturgy as recognized in the thirteenth century, extending from Easter through Pentecost: two for Easter, one for Ascension, two for Pentecost. In these motets, Christ's self-sacrifice and related paschal messages intersect in varying ways with the *malmariée* topos.

Both Easter motets are built upon the tenor incipit *IMMOLATUS* from the Easter *Alleluia. Pascha nostrum immolatus est Christus* (Alleluia. Christ our Passover has been sacrificed for us) (M14); both invite a parodic reading in relationship to that chant fragment.

In **Mo** 6, 203, *Hier main jouer m'en alai* (238)/*[IMMO]LATUS* (M14), the motetus adopts the encounter frame from a *pastourelle*, revealing a narrator who relates having overheard a conversation between a married couple:

Motetus
Hier main jouer m'en alai,
tous seuz parmi une pree
chevauchai.
La truis dame quellant glai;
gentement fu acesmee,
ceur ot gai.
Vers le ma voie tornai;
lés li son mari trovai.
D'amours la forment blasmee;
Ele respont sans delai:
"*Voz dirés,*   vdB 1856
ce que vous vaudrez,
mes j'amerai!"

(Yesterday morning I went off all alone in search of distraction. As I galloped through a meadow, I found there a lady gathering lilies; she was finely dressed and had a gay heart. I turned toward her; beside her, her husband I found. He strongly criticized her for loving, but she responded without hesitation: "*You can say what you want, but I will continue to love!*")

The narrator relates that the husband criticized his wife "for loving," which she says she will continue to do (see refrain vdB 1856). This love, clearly outside of marriage, is presumably adulterous. Based on this assumption, we consider the text's resonance with the tenor *IMMOLATUS*. The Alleluia verse opening where *IMMOLATUS* appears emphasizes Christ's sacrificial act rather than His Resurrection per se. The focus on personal immolation invites a parodic reading: the motetus foregrounds a married woman who, confronted with expectations for marital fidelity, clearly refuses to forgo her erotic desires, thereby setting up a contrast between her focus on self-fulfillment and Christ's actions on behalf of others. Scholars such as Linda Hutcheon and Sylvia Huot have interpreted the relationship between the parodic foreground and parodied background text as dialogic, "whose irony can cut both ways," that is, the parodied text is not necessarily the target of the irony. In the case of Mo 6, 203, a listener could hear the motetus as an irreverent take on the tenor's sincere message of self-sacrifice, or view the contrast as highlighting "the frivolity or pretentiousness of the upper voice," that is, the *malmariée* becomes the object of mockery.[1] Here and throughout its pages, when this study attributes a parodic character to a motet's *malmariée* voice, it implicitly acknowledges the very real possibility of bi-directional irony.

Might we also consider an allegorical reading in which the women's statement "I will continue to love" relates to a spiritual love? This possibility seems unlikely because the *dame* (lady) is introduced as having a *ceur ot gai* (gay heart), a sentiment often attributed to individuals pursuing earthly love in vernacular lyrics.[2]

---

1 In *Allegorical Play in the Old French Motet: The Sacred and the Profane in Thirteenth-Century Polyphony* (Stanford, CA: Stanford University Press, 1997), 12–13, Sylvia Huot summarizes Hutcheon's view, as well as that of Mikhail Bakhtin.

2 See the *malmariée* motet to be discussed below: **Mo 5**, 148, where married women speak, using this phrase or a variant of it: the first "was moved by a gay heart to sing" (*l'une s'esmut de cuer gai a chanter*), and the second "and then with a joyous heart" (*puis a dit de cuer joious*), both followed by refrains about pursuing love with a sweetheart. See also **Mo 6**, 237: "when I no longer have a gay heart" (*quant nus mes n'a le cuer gai*), whose speaker is arguing with himself about whether to cease singing because of "evil ones," presumably the slanderers who report on his

Another likely reading of this motet relies upon its interplay among song types discussed by Susan M. Johnson,[3] whereby an audience's experience of a new work would have rested on knowing conventions associated with various song types that had been codified in France in the thirteenth century. Playing with song type expectations could be an effective way to engage one's audience intellectually, perhaps to elicit surprise and/or humor. As Sylvia Huot has noted, the vernacular motet genre reveals an "intellectual playfulness [that] is reflected in its innovative expansions on vernacular lyric and its mixing of languages and traditions."[4] Thus, looking beyond the *malmariée*'s parody of the tenor message, **Mo** 6, 203 begins with an encounter framework familiar from the *pastourelle*. What follows sets expectations on their heel because the narrator happens not upon a shepherdess, but a finely dressed woman and her husband. The defiance usually voiced by a shepherdess in such an encounter is here attributed to a presumably higher-class married woman, as suggested by the descriptor "finely dressed." The motet thus invites a listener's recognition of its intergeneric play.[5] One wonders, might it also have suggested that women's character traits cannot be neatly segregated by social class?

The second Easter-related motet on *IMMOLATUS* is **Mo** 6, 180, *A tort sui d'amours blasmee* (241)/[*IMMO*]*LATUS* (M14). Only its opening refrain aligns it with the *malmariée* topos: vdB 189 *A tort sui d'amours blasmee, hé Dieus, si n'ai point d'ami!* (I am wrongly criticized for loving. Alas, I have no lover!). This refrain appears within a *chanson avec des refrains*, *Quant se resjoïssent oisel*, transmitted in four thirteenth-century sources, one of which attributes it to Thibaut de Blaison (see Chapter 5 for discussion of transmission). This chanson mentions a husband (*mari*) in four of its seven verses; verse 1 ends with vdB 189, in which the married woman denies having a lover:

> Quant se resjoïssent oisel
> Au tens que je voi renverdir,
> Vi deus dames soz un chastel
> Floretes en un prè coillir.
> La plus jone se gaimentoit,

---

amorous intentions. I have not found the expression in motets that allegorize the Virgin Mary.
3 See note 2 in the introductory pages of Part I.
4 Huot, *Allegorical Play*, 10–11.
5 See discussion of this motet by Grau, "Representation and Resistance: Female Vocality in Thirteenth-Century France," 18–20.

A l'ainneie se li disoit:
"Dame, conseil vos quier et pri
De mon mari qui me mescroit,
Et se n'i a encore nul droit,
C'onques d'amors n'oi fors lo cri."
A tort sui d'amors blasmeie,   vdB 189
Lasse! Si n'ai point d'ami.[6]

The motet's upper-voice text begins with the same refrain, slightly varied:

A tort sui d'amours blasmee;   vdB 189
hé, Dieus, si n'ai point d'ami!
Pour ce me sui j'a celle donee,
qui mere est celuis, qui
por noz en la crois mort souffri;
de touz doit estre henouree.
Si li cri merci
a jointes mains et pri,
qu'el ne me mete en oubli, si
qu'a s'amour n'aie failli.

(*I am wrongly criticized for loving. O God, I have no lover!* Thus have I given myself to the mother of Him who suffered death for us on the cross; she should be honored by all. I cry to her for mercy, and with folded hands I pray that she not forget me so that I not lack her love.)

Apart from its refrain, the motetus text is in effect a *chanson pieuse*, addressed to the Virgin Mary. The woman declares her devotion to Mary, crying and praying that Mary grant her mercy and love. More directly than in **Mo 6, 203**, the issue of Christ's sacrifice for mankind encapsulated in the tenor *IMMOLATUS* is evoked through the woman's words "I have given myself to the mother of Him who suffered death for us on the cross." The speaker elevates her personal dedication to Mary through the allusion to Christ's sacrifice. But what is the effect of beginning with words uttered elsewhere by an unhappily married woman denying that she has a lover? To a listener familiar with the refrain from the *chanson avec des refrains*, hearing it followed

---

6 For full text, see *Chanter m'estuet: Songs of the Trouvères*, ed. S. N. Rosenberg, music ed. H. Tischler (Bloomington: Indiana University Press, 1981), 279–82, which classifies the work as a *chanson de rencontre*.

by a statement of devotion to Mary may suggest a parodic juxtaposition of seeming self-sacrifice: an unhappily married woman *not* taking a lover versus a woman dedicating herself to Mary. Thus, the opening *malmariée* refrain takes part in a multi-pronged play on the subject of self-sacrifice: an unhappily married woman who claims not to have sought satisfaction by taking a lover parodies a woman dedicating herself to Mary, while in turn the holy woman's self-sacrifice allegorizes Christ's sacrifice encapsulated in the tenor fragment.

The single Ascension motet, **Mo** 2, 23, *Dame, que j'aim et desir* (334)/ *Amors vaint tot fors cuer de felon* (335)/*Au tans d'esté, que cil oisel* (336)/ *ET GAUDEBIT* (M24), offers a rich array of readings through the interaction of its four voices, primarily involving parody, but allowing one allegorical reading as well. The motet's *malmariée* sentiments lie in the triplum, which begins with a twenty-four-line encomium of love and its effects (including the gift of song) on individuals who love. At line 20, the focus switches from the male to the *malmariée*:

et (a) amour
fait par douçor
dame amer autresi,
et son mal mari
guiler et chanter a haut cri:

(And Love, because of his sweetness, makes a lady love another and deceive her nasty husband and sing at the top of her lungs:)

There follows an extended first-person address by a discontented wife who has found true love with someone other than her husband; she utters six refrains within lines 25–41:

> **(1-vdB 587)**, lines 25–27: *Doleroz mari, vous ne savrés hui, qui amiete je sui.* (*Sorrowful husband, you will not know today whose sweetheart I am.*) Also in **Mo** 5, 142.
> **(2-vdB 286)**, lines 28–29: *Bon jour et hennor ait mon ami.* (*May my lover have happiness and honor.*)
> line 30: Si prierai et pri: (And so I will pray, and do now pray:)
> **(3-vdB 900)**: lines 31–33: *Ja Dieus ne me doinst corage d'amer mon mari, tant com j'avrai ami;* (*May God never give me the desire to love my husband as long as I have a lover;*) also in **Mo** 5, 142.
> **(4-vdB 971)**, lines 34–35: *J'ai plus chier un dous baisier de li que le solas mon mari.* (*I hold dearer one sweet kiss from him than the solace of my husband.*)
> line 36: Si chanterai: (And I will sing:)

(5-vdB 664), lines 37–38: *En non Diu, amors me tienent, ja n'en garirai;* (*In the name of God, Love has me in his grip and never will I be cured;*)
(6-vdB 748), lines 39–41: *Fines amouretes ai et bel ami joli, dont ja ne partirai.* (*I have true love and a handsome, gay lover from whom I will never part.*)

The triplum's collective mentions of a handsome, gay lover, "true love" in opposition to marital love, and even the wife's explicit wish that God not guide her to love her husband, all contribute to a depiction of a defiant woman, determined to satisfy her desire for love outside of marriage. The woman's brazen tone contrasts directly with the principled sentiment expressed by the quadruplum's male speaker: he links love to loyalty, honor, and worth, going so far as to claim: *tot bien en vient et tot enseignement* (all good comes from [love], and all knowledge). He refers to the negative side of his distanced love experience only at the end: *que je sai bien, que tout a mon talent me merira et donra aliegement cele, qui j'aim et reclaim de cuer entierement* (for I know well that she whom I love and entreat with my entire heart will reward me and relieve my pain exactly as I desire). In effect, the male speaker downplays the usual pained expressions of the *grand chant courtois*, and instead idealizes love and the woman whom he desires. A listener might interpret the *malmariée* who acts on her desire for love as a parody of the male who sits and waits, loving only in his imagination.[7] At the same time, the woman's openness to an adulterous relationship could be interpreted as empowering him: she is the embodiment of his male fantasy.

The triplum also contrasts with the tenor, but obliquely through the motetus, a *chanson d'ami*, which begins with an encounter frame: a male passerby overhears a woman lamenting her loved one's absence: *Biaus doz amis, trop m'avés mis en grief pensee, ce m'est vis, trop m'avés obliee!* (Fair, sweet beloved, you have indeed grieved me—in my opinion, you have completely forgotten me!). In response, the passerby tries to comfort her and promises not to depart: vdB 1778 *Tos jors vos servirai ne ja de vos ne partirai* (I will always serve you and never from you shall I part). The ideas of departure and comfort are fundamental

---

7 This contrast also seems to play out within the motetus text itself: its introductory encomium of Love first describes its effects on "lads" (*jolis*) and on composition of *chanson, dit, conductus,* and *virelai*—presumably associated with male creators, then switches to how Love affects a *malmariée*. The male composes songs about love, while the woman acts on love.

to the tenor from which *ET GAUDEBIT* is taken: *Alleluia. Non vos relinquam orphanos* (M24). This Ascension Alleluia foregrounds Christ's reassuring words to His disciples in anticipation of His death, "I will not leave you orphans" (*orphanos* is sometimes read as "comfortless"), followed by His promise of return, "I will come back to you, and your hearts will be full of joy." These last words prefigure the consoling presence of the Holy Spirit at Pentecost. Thus, the offer of comfort by the male speaker of the motetus and his promise not to depart can be read as an allegory of the tenor message spoken by Christ.[8] But when the triplum's married woman claims she will not depart from *her loved one* in refrain vdB 748 *Fines amouretes ai et bel ami joli, dont ja ne partirai*, sounded simultaneously with the motetus's vdB 1778, the clear context of adultery suggests a parody of the motetus sentiment, and in turn of the tenor. An allegorical interpretation of the *malmariée* does not seem possible.

Two *malmariée* motets use two different Pentecost tenor chants with nuanced meanings of divine love. The M27 incipit *AMORIS* is taken from *Alleluia. Veni sancte spiritus, reple tuorum corda fidelium, et tua amoris in eis ignem accende.* (Alleluia. Come, Holy Spirit, fill the hearts of your faithful ones, and kindle the fire of your love in them). The tenor *AMORIS* thus brings to mind the Pentecostal image of the Holy Spirit sparking a fire within us through his love, inspiring us to make that love grow. The M26 incipit *DOCEBIT* is taken from another Pentecost chant, *Alleluia. Paraclitus spiritus sanctus, quem mittet pater in nomine meo, ille vos docebit omnem veritatem.* (Alleluia. The Comforter, the Holy Spirit, which the father will send in my name, he will teach you every truth). Within these words spoken by Christ about the Holy Spirit as Comforter, *DOCEBIT* implies a different sort of love, one that replenishes and edifies us, even in the face of loss.

When each of these Pentecost fragments focused on love is paired with a *malmariée* motetus, the resulting two-voice motet suggests allegory and, in one case, parody as well. The allegory in both motets engages the idea of a woman refusing earthly marriage and allying

---

8 For discussion of the broader allegorical contexts for *ET GAUDEBIT*, see Gerald R. Hoekstra, "The French Motet as Trope: Multiple Levels of Meaning in *Quant florist la violete/El mois de mai/Et gaudebit*," *Speculum* 73 (1998): 32–57; and Rebecca Baltzer, "The Polyphonic Progeny of an *Et gaudebit*: Assessing Family Relations in the Thirteenth-Century Motet," in *Hearing the Motet: Essays on the Motet of the Middle Ages and Renaissance*, ed. Dolores Pesce (New York and Oxford: Oxford University Press, 1997), 17–27.

herself instead to a heavenly Bridegroom as she makes a religious profession.

The motetus text of EM 310, *Ja ne mi marierai* (367)/*AMORIS* (M27), consists of these words spoken by a woman: vdB 1006 *Ja ne mi marierai, més par amors amerai.* vdB 1374 *Ne vos mariez mie, tenez vous ensi* (Never will I marry; rather, I will love. Do not marry, keep yourself this way). She speaks against marriage, but in favor of love. Though the sort of love is not specified, two readings are possible in the context of a woman privileging love. One implies a desire for extramarital love, grounded in a view that marriage is often loveless. In this reading, the motetus parodies the spiritual sentiment of the tenor *AMORIS* that expresses a wish for divine love brought by the Holy Spirit. The second reading focuses on a woman's decision to refuse marriage and instead consecrate herself to God—a real possibility for some women in the period under consideration. In this case, the love favored in the motetus text can be read as a symbol for the inspirational love of the Holy Spirit, leading to a chaste and holy life.[9]

The second Pentecost tenor *DOCEBIT* is paired in **Mo** 6, 243, *Pour quoi m'avés voz douné* (353)/*DOCEBIT* (M26), with a motetus whose female speaker derides the concept of arranged marriage. The girl reproaches her mother for forcing her to marry someone other than the one she loves, using vdB 1514 *Pour quoi m'avés voz douné, mere, mari? Ja saviés vous [bien], qu'avoie ami!* (Why have you given me, mother, a husband? You knew well enough that I had a sweetheart!). A secularized reading of the tenor incipit *DOCEBIT* (he/she will teach) might imply that love (or even the mother) will instruct the young woman of the motetus on how to keep her lover, even while married.[10] An allegorical reading of the motetus text, on the other hand, again offers the possibility of a woman having pledged herself to a heavenly Bridegroom, that is, having refused earthly marriage in favor of a celibate life. In this reading, the motetus speaker, facing a forced marriage, looks to the Holy Spirit for comfort and edifying love.

In summary, the five paschal season motets bring the *malmariée* into dialogue with the tenor messages of Christ's sacrifice, His comforting promise of return, and the fulfillment of that promise through the intercession of the Holy Spirit. The treatment tends toward the parodic, especially in the two motets on the Easter-related *IMMOLATUS*,

---

9 Of course, the tenor *amoris* may have been chosen for its most general meaning of "love," interpreted in this context as human love.
10 Huot, Allegorical Play, 109.

which contrast the unhappily married woman, who may or may not take a lover, with the self-sacrificing Christ. In the two motets on Pentecost tenors *AMORIS* and *DOCEBIT*, which convey respectively the inspirational and comforting love of the Holy Spirit, the *malmariée*'s protest against marriage but in favor of love can be read as an allegory of a woman consecrating herself to God and, in one case, also as a parodic embrace of extramarital love. The Ascension motet reveals multiple levels of parody as the triplum's defiant *malmariée* contrasts with the idealizing male lover of the triplum, the comforting male of the motetus, and the selfless Christ of the tenor.

2 Assumption Liturgy

The feast of the Assumption celebrates Mary being taken into Heaven at the end of her earthly life to reign as Queen of Heaven with Christ. As depicted in the Mass entrance antiphon, her image is that of Revelation 12: 1: "a woman clothed with the sun, and the moon beneath her feet, and on her head a crown of twelve stars." This exalted position follows from her role as Mother of God. According to the Assumption Gospel text, Luke 1: 39–56, Mary revels in God choosing her to bear His Son. Her ready acceptance of God's call and her inviolate conception of Christ warrant her assumption into Heaven "as the beginning and image of your Church's coming to Perfection" (Assumption Preface). Simply put, her selfless acceptance of God's will and her devotion to Christ are models for those who seek God's salvation. Mary becomes their heavenly intercessor (Prayer over the Offerings).

Five motets in this corpus are based on Assumption-related tenors: two (**Mo** 5, 156, **Mo** 5, 169) on *VERITATEM*, taken from the Gradual *Propter veritatem. Audi filia*, for the Assumption (M37)[1]; and three (**Mo** 6, 233, **Mo** 5, 142, **Mo** 5, 148) on *PORTARE* (M22), taken from the *Alleluia. Dulcis virgo, dulcis mater*, for the octave of the Assumption. The overriding liturgical message of these Assumption chants is of Mary's devotion to Christ as she becomes his heavenly Bride. The *malmariée* of the motets, determined to find personal gratification, parodies the selfless Mary.

---

1 Catherine Bradley, *Polyphony in Medieval Paris: The Art of Composing with Plainchant* (Cambridge: Cambridge University Press, 2018), 13, notes that *Propter veritatem* was also sung on the feast of Mary's Nativity (September 8) in a number of French cathedrals, and included within the common liturgy for other female saints in Parisian chant books.

The Assumption Gradual *Propter veritatem*. *Audi filia* draws on Psalm 44,[2] which is viewed as a wedding song written to a king on the day of his marriage to a foreign woman. Christian scholars frequently interpret the psalm's imagery as a prophecy of Jesus as both the future king and Bridegroom of the Church, that is, the psalm evokes a mystical marriage. The Assumption Gradual adapts the psalm's verses 5 and 11–12, which address the woman: *Propter veritatem, et mansuetudinem, et justitiam: et duducet te mirabiliter dextera tua. V. Audi, filia, et vide, et inclina aurem tuam: quia concupivit rex speciem tuam.* (For truth, and mercy, and justice: and he shall lead you marvelously by your right hand. V. Hear daughter, and see, and incline your ear: for the king has desired your beauty). When these lines sound in the Assumption liturgy, a listener may reflect on Mary as Christ's heavenly Bride. In turn, when the chant is heard in a *malmariée* motet context, it invites comparisons of its spiritual bride with the married woman featured in the upper-voice texts.

The first of the *VERITATEM* motets is **Mo** 5, 156, *Je sui jonete et jolie* (465)/*Hé Dieus, je n'ai pas mari* (466)/*VERITATEM* (M37). Both upper-voice texts are in the voice of the *malmariée:*

Triplum
Je sui jonete et jolie;
s'ai un cuer enamoré,
qui tant mi semont et prie
d'amer par jolieté,
que tuit i sunt mi pensé.
Mes mon mari ne set mie,
a qui j'ai mon cuer doné;
par les Sains, que l'en deprie,
il morroit de jalousie,

---

2 A metrical paraphrase of Psalm 44 in French was written between 1181 and 1187 and copied as late as the fifteenth century. See T. Atkinson Jenkins, ed., *Eructavit: An Old French Metrical Paraphrase of Psalm XLIV Published from All the Known Manuscripts and Attributed to Adam de Perseigne* (Dresden: Die Gesellschaft für romanische Literature, 1909). The work is dedicated to *ma dame de Champaigne*, thought to be Marie, Countess of Champagne. According to Jenkins, xxix–xxxi, of the surviving fourteen manuscripts, ten are dated to the thirteenth century, of which four suggest ties to northern France: Paris, Bibliothèque Ste.-Geneviève L (Picard traits); Paris, Bibliothèque de l'Arsenal 3518 (Picard traits); Paris, Arsenal 3516 (written about 1265 in Artois); Paris, BnF fr. 1536 (written in the extreme north). Paris, BnF fr. 25532, probably from St-Médard de Soissons, approximately sixty miles northeast of Paris, also transmits the paraphrase.

s'il savoit la verité.
Mes, foi que je doi a Dé,
j'amerai;
ja pour mari ne lairai!
Quant il fait tout a son gré
et de mon cors sa volenté,
del plus mon plesir ferai.

(I am young and pretty and have an enamored heart that urges and beseeches me so much to love gaily that all my thoughts are of love. But my husband knows not to whom I have given my heart. By the saints above he would die of jealousy if he knew the truth. But, by the faith I owe to God, I will love; never will I cease because of a husband. When he does all he would and has his pleasure from my body, all the more will I do as I please.)

Motetus
Hé Dieus, je n'ai pas mari
du tot a mon gré:
Il n'a cortoisie en li
ne joliveté.
Jone dame est bien traïe,
par la foi que doi a Dé,
qui a vilain est baillie
pour faire sa volonté;
ce fu trop mal devisé.
De mari sui mal païe,
d'ami m'en amenderai;
et se m'en savoit mal gré
mon mari, si face amie,
car, voelle ou non, j'amerai.

(O God, my husband is not at all to my liking: there is no courtesy or merriment in him. By the faith I owe to God, a young lady is indeed betrayed when she is bound over to a villain to do with as he would; this was surely ill-arranged. Since I am poorly rewarded in my husband, I will make up for it with a lover. And if my husband is resentful, let him find a sweetheart, for whether he like it or not, I will love.)

According to Sylvia Huot, because the Gradual *Propter veritatem* alludes to the prospective bride's appearance ("the king has desired her beauty"), vernacular motets on this tenor reflect "irresistible opportunities for parodic secularization inherent in the liturgical expression of desire for a beautiful girl."[3] In this motet, the triplum perhaps relates to the tenor in this way when the woman refers to herself as "young and pretty," but otherwise her defiant, self-focused persona in both upper voices offers a parodic contrast to the selfless Virgin celebrated in the Assumption liturgy. On another level, these upper-voice texts allude to marriage realities in the thirteenth century. In the motetus a woman refers to her husband as a *vilain* (a term to be discussed further below), the marriage as "ill-arranged," and states her decision to take a lover; in the triplum, a married woman declares that she has already taken a lover:

> But my husband knows not to whom I have given my heart....
> I will love; never will I cease because of a husband. When he does all he would and has his pleasure from my body, all the more will I do as I please.

In short, the texts refer to arranged marriages, marital debt, and a married woman's decision to work around those strictures and fulfill her own desires. She is anything but selfless.

The second *VERITATEM* motet, **Mo** 5, 169, *Li jalous par tout son fustat* (467)/*Tuit cil qui sunt enamourat* (468)/*VERITATEM* (M37), stands apart in the corpus because it does not present a female voice, let alone that of a married woman. Instead, both upper-voice texts suggest a third-person point-of-view (emphasis added):

Triplum
Li **jalous** par tout sunt fustat
et **portent corne en mi le front**;
par tout doivent estre huat.
La regine le commendat,
que d'un baston soient frapat
et chacié hors comme larron.
S'en dançade veillent entrar,
fier le[s] du pie comme garçon.

(Everywhere the **jealous** are thrashed and **wear a horn in the middle of their foreheads**; they should be jeered by everyone. The queen commands that they be beaten with a stick and driven away like thieves.

---

3 Huot, *Allegorical Play*, 99.

If they want to take part in the dancing, kick them with your foot as you would a boy.)

Motetus
Tuit cil qui sunt enamourat   vdB 1822
viegnent dançar, li autre non.
La regine le commendat
(tuit cil qui sunt enamourat),
que li **jalous** soient fustat
fors de la dance d'un baston.
Tuit cil qui sunt enamourat
viegnent avant, li autre non.

(*All of those who are in love may come and dance, but not the others.* The queen commands (*all those who are in love*) that the **jealous** be driven away from the dance with a stick. *All those who are in love may come forward, but not the others.*)

The boldfaced words associate these paired texts with the *malmariée* topos by suggesting a jealous husband whose wife has cuckolded him. Determining how listeners may have interpreted this image within the texts as a whole requires an examination of three contexts: May fests, the source of the motetus refrain vdB 1822, and Psalm 44, from which the tenor *VERITATEM* derives. Sylvia Huot's work in particular informs the following discussion.[4]

As discussed in the Introduction, Jeanroy theorized that women composed songs, probably in combination with dance, for May fests (*maieroles* or *fêtes de mai*). He claimed that the earliest songs were essentially *chansons de malmariée*, in view of the fact that the *maieroles* "often featured a May Queen who led the dance with her female companions, excluding the *gelos*—the husband and all those who did not love."[5] Huot attributes these particular motet texts to this tradition, claiming they draw from the repertory of "songs of May and dance songs where love is freely expressed and where women are not afraid to proclaim their amorous desire or dissatisfaction with their husbands."[6]

Huot further notes that the motetus refrain vdB 1822, "All of those who are in love may come and dance, but not the others," appears in

---

4 Ibid., especially 78–80 and 103–6.
5 See Introduction, note 26.
6 Huot, *Allegorical Play*, 104.

La Court de Paradis,[7] a short anonymous poem of 642 lines written at the end of the thirteenth century. According to Huot,

> This short thirteenth-century poem describes **a carol held in Heaven**; Christ, flanked by Mary Magdalene and the Virgin, presides over the festivities. **All the souls of the saved participate**, arriving in groups according to their status: Old Testament prophets, martyrs, confessors, virgins, and so on. As each group joins in the dance, its members sing an amorous refrain that corresponds, at least generally, to that group's identity and participation in divine love; ...[8] (emphasis added)

The highlighted expressions invite examination. The carol or carole was a type of revelry involving song and dance, popular in the twelfth and thirteenth centuries, attended by young clerics and students, as well as townspeople and courtiers.[9] Church leaders heaped invective on the carole because they viewed it as cultivating earthly pleasures, including song, dance, and amorous pursuits, at the expense of spiritual salvation.[10] Huot outlines a number of literary responses to the Church's belief in the irreconcilability of earthly and sacred pursuits, including the idea of a heavenly carole, found in a number of texts but particularly in *La Court de Paradis*.[11] In this poem, Heaven becomes the setting for a carole whose participants sing vernacular refrains that now function as expressions of love for Christ. At the poem's opening, Mary, the Queen of Heaven, invites all amorous souls to dance in the heavenly carole, as she sings refrain vdB 1822. The separation of lovers and non-lovers inherent in the refrain seems to transfer in *La Court de Paradis* to the distinction between the saved and the damned, as Huot's highlighted phrase above suggests: "all the souls of the saved participate." This understanding brings us back to the idea of the May fest from which jealous husbands were banned, because the wives considered them unable to truly love. Thus, within *La Court de Paradis*, Mary as the Queen of Heaven may be equated with the May

---

7 For an edition, see Eva Vilamo-Pentti, ed., *La Court de Paradis, poème anonyme du XIIIe siècle* (Helsinki: Société de Littérature Finnoise, 1953).
8 Huot, *Allegorical Play*, 78.
9 Ibid., 6.
10 Christopher Page, *The Owl and the Nightingale: Musical Life and Ideas in France 1100–1300* (Berkeley: University of California Press, 1990), ch. 5, pp. 110–33: "The *Carole*, the Pulpit and the Schools."
11 See Huot, *Allegorical Play*, 14–18 and 77–84.

Queen who presides over the festivities and determines who is worthy to participate, a category in which jealous husbands do not belong.

Reading the motet texts in relationship to the idea of a heavenly carole, which is linked in turn to a May fest that excludes jealous husbands, provides one somewhat literal interpretation. But others arise when one considers the texts in the context of the Assumption. The motetus's invitation to lovers recalls the summons to the Beloved in the Song of Songs, a summons that reverberates in the Assumption *Alleluia. Veni electa mea* (M54) that is used on the first three days of the octave: *Veni electa mea et ponam te in thronum meum, quia concupivit rex speciem tuam.* (Come, my chosen one, and I will place you upon my throne, for the king has desired your beauty). *Alleluia. Veni electa mea* is derived from Psalm 44, as is the Gradual *Propter veritatem.* As noted above, Psalm 44 is founded on nuptial imagery of a king about to marry a foreign woman. When used in the context of the Assumption liturgy, *VERITATEM* brings to mind the mystical marriage of Mary and Christ upon her arrival in Heaven. By juxtaposing the secular celebration of love in the motet texts to a *VERITATEM* tenor, the motet creator invites several interpretations. According to Huot, one might hear a humorous contrast between the two, or consider the motet texts as an allegorical representation of the mystical marriage.[12] The latter requires imagining the festive dance depicted in the motet texts as a nuptial celebration, which may be possible for some listeners. Nonetheless, this study offers the following refinement of Huot's interpretations. The motet texts may evoke a May fest that excludes jealous husbands, possibly bringing to mind the heavenly carole in *La Court de Paradis*, which excludes those who do not love. Second, the juxtaposition of the secular love celebration in the upper-voice texts with that of the mystical love celebration in the tenor may be heard as a parody. Furthermore, because the motet texts refer to the dissatisfied, jealous husband, that image by extension brings into focus the devoted Bridegroom of the tenor, and thus a more specific level of parody arises.[13]

In sum, the present study includes this motet even if it does not feature the discontented wife directly. Its allusion to jealous, cuckolded husbands who are excluded from a festive celebration, contrasting

---

12 Ibid., 106.
13 Ibid. Huot concludes somewhat differently, after her statement about both literal (humorous) and allegorical readings: "The present example retains its element of humor; the two levels of meaning are resolved, ultimately, when we understand it as parodic allegory."

with the tenor's evocation of a mystical marriage, may bring to mind a *malmariée* nonetheless.

Three motets are built upon the tenor *PORTARE* (M22). This incipit, used interchangeably with *sustinere*, offers Christological and Marian resonances because of its dual liturgical associations with the Feasts of the Holy Cross and the Assumption.[14] The texts dignify the Cross and Mary as worthy to bear the weight of Christ:

> *Alleluia. Dulce lignum, dulces claves, dulcia ferens pondera, que sola fuisti digna sustinere regem celorum et Dominum.*
> (Alleluia. Sweet wood, sweet nails, bearing the sweet weight, you alone were worthy of bearing the Lord, king of heaven.)
>
> *Alleluia. Dulcis virgo, dulcis mater, dulcia ferens pondera, que sola fuisti digna portare regem celorum et Dominum.*
> (Alleluia. Sweet virgin, sweet mother, bearing the sweet weight, you alone were worthy of carrying the Lord, king of heaven.)

That Mary was present at the foot of the Cross adds a more nuanced meaning to her association with this tenor incipit: she joyfully bore Christ, but also stood at the foot of the Cross, participating in the sorrow of His Crucifixion. The final image within the tenor nexus of ideas is that of Mary's assumption into Heaven, where she is joyfully reunited with Christ to become His heavenly Bride.[15] Mary's devotion to Christ is paramount in all these images, and serves as an integral concept in the motets based on *PORTARE*.

---

14 Dolores Pesce, "Beyond Glossing: The Old Made New in *Mout me fu grief/Robin m'aime/PORTARE*," in *Hearing the Motet: Essays on the Motet of the Middle Ages and Renaissance*, ed. Dolores Pesce (New York and Oxford: Oxford University Press, 1997), 37–44.

15 In his study *Medieval Marriage: Symbolism and Society* (Oxford and New York: Oxford University Press, 2005), pp. 201-2, David d'Avray comments on the various ways that the symbols of bride and bridegroom are used within Christian writings:

> The Church as bride of Christ is composed of men as well as women. The soul as bride of Christ is the soul of a man as much as the soul of a woman. The bride can stand for Christ and the bridegroom for the Church. This in itself diminishes the impact of the symbolism on real gender relations. Furthermore, the point of the symbolism analysed throughout this book is not about gender specificity so much as unity and indissolubility.

In the context of motets, however, symbols function in relationship to a chant incipit that is associated with a specific liturgical feast day, such as *PORTARE* with the Assumption of Mary. In this case, the image of Mary as Bride of Christ creates a female gendering of the motet as a whole.

36 Malmariée *Motets in Relationship to Their Tenors*

In the first example, **Mo** 6, 233, *Hyer main chevauchoie* (273)/*PORTARE* (M22), the motetus again uses an encounter frame, familiar from the *pastourelle*, and therefore sets up generic expectations that are thwarted by what follows. Instead of a shepherdess, the narrator relates what he overhears spoken by a *malmariée* who believes she is alone. The full text reads:

> Hyer main chevauchoie
> dejouste un vergier flori;
> bele joenne j'ai choisi,
> qui cuide, que nus ne l'oise.
> Si se plaint du dangier son mari
> et dit seri:
> "*Se j'osoie,*   vdB 1691
> *ge feroie ami.*"

(Yesterday morning I was riding by an orchard in bloom when I espied a fair maiden who thought that no one heard her. She complained of the domination of her husband and spoke sweetly: "*If I dared, I would take a lover.*")

In the context of a complaint against her husband's treatment, the *malmariée*'s words "take a lover" imply a real action on her part in retaliation against her husband. Accordingly, it seems less likely that the motetus on its own would be read allegorically as an imagined embracing of a spiritual Bridegroom. What about in association with the tenor *PORTARE*? A parodic interpretation is possible: the woman's less than wholehearted engagement in her marriage contrasts with the intense devotion of Mary to Christ epitomized in the tenor.

Finally, this motetus text may invite a listener's reflection on female and male fantasies: the *malmariée* would like to fulfill her fantasy of taking a lover, but is fearful. In turn, her wistful statement could play into a male fantasy of finding a willing female lover.

Mo 5, 142, *Nus ne set les biens d'amors* (286)/*Ja Dieus ne me doinst corage* (287)/*PORTARE* (M22), presents an entire motetus text devoted to the voice of the *malmariée*, her speech framed by the two refrains (vdB 900 and 587) shared with **Mo** 2, 23 (discussed in Chapter 1):

> *Ja Dieus ne me doinst corage*   vdB 900
> *d'amer mon mari,*
> *tant com je aie ami,*
> *tel com je l'ai choisi,*
> *preu et vaillant et joli,*

deduisant, cortois et sage.
Mes li miens maris s'errage
de savoir son grant damage;
si veut savoir, qui
j'ai doné de m'amor gaige.
Je li respondi:
"Fi, vilains au fol visage!   vdB 587
Vous ne sarés hui,
qui amiete je sui."

(*May God never grant me the desire to love my husband as long as I have a sweetheart* like the one I have chosen: noble and worthy and brave, amusing and courteous and careful. Knowledge of his great misfortune enrages my husband; he wants to know to whom I have pledged my love. I answered him: *"Fie, villain with the madly contorted face! It is not today that you will know whose sweetheart I am."*)

As was true in **Mo** 2, 23, the woman speaks in defiance of her husband and in favor of love outside of her marriage. Refrain vdB 587 now begins with the strongly worded "Fie, villain with the madly contorted face!" instead of the milder "Sorrowful husband" found in **Mo** 2, 23. Furthermore, whereas in **Mo** 2, 23, the wife's rhetoric interacted somewhat obliquely with the tenor message of *ET GAUDEBIT* about Christ promising to return and offer comfort, in Mo **5**, 142, her words sounding over the *PORTARE* chant invite a direct parodic interpretation related to the overall message of the Assumption liturgy. As in the *PORTARE* motet **Mo** 6, 233, the *malmariée* of **Mo** 5, 142, who finds discontent in her spousal relationship, parodies the liturgy's message of Mary as Christ's devoted Bride.

We recall that the *malmariée* triplum voice of **Mo** 2, 23 contrasted with its quadruplum voice that featured a male idealizing love in the tradition of the *grand chant courtois*. The same contrast can be found in **Mo** 5, 142 where the male speaker of its triplum concentrates on the ennobling effects of loving a woman despite love's sorrow and pains, whereas the unhappy wife of the motetus seeks an immediate, *consummated* love with a man who happens not to be her husband. In contrast to the idealized love professed by the male speaker of the triplum, the *malmariée* "redefines love as adultery."[16] Thus, the motetus parodies the tenor's invocation of a spiritually grounded spousal love, and also the trouvère model of idealized love from afar. At the same time,

---

16 Huot, *Allegorical Play*, 26.

because the *malmariée* attributes to her lover the desirable personal traits of a male in the *grand chant courtois* tradition—*preu et vaillant et joli, deduisant, cortois et sage* (noble and worthy and brave, amusing and courteous and careful), the juxtaposition of motetus and triplum might also be read as empowering a male within a courtly setting as he fantasizes about attaining an ostensibly unattainable woman.

A third *PORTARE* motet is **Mo** 5, 148, *Si com<e> aloie jouer* (288)/ *Deduisant com fins amourous* (289)/*PORTARE* (M22). Its two texts are conceived together, both using an encounter frame in which a male passes by three ladies, whose conversation he relates:

Triplum
Si com<e> aloie jouer
l'autrier, trois dames trovai.
L'une s'esmut de cuer gai
a chanter:
"*Dieus, je n'i os aler*   vdB 532
a mon ami!
Coment avrai merci?"
Puis a dit tout sanz delai:
"*Fines amouretes ai trovees,*   vdB 750
bien seront gaitees."
Puis a dit de cuer joious:
"*Pleüst a Dieu, que chascune de nous*   vdB 1489
tenist la pieau de son mari jalous
et mes doz [amis] fust avec moi!
Touz li cuers me rit de joie, quant le voi; vdB 1781
du tout a lui m'otroi."

(As I went out to amuse myself the other day, I found three ladies. One was moved by a gay heart to sing: "*God, I dare not go to my sweetheart! How shall I have mercy?*" Then with nary a pause: "*I have found true love and I will keep watch over it.*" And then with a joyous heart: "*May it please God that each of us have the skin of her jealous husband*; would that my sweetheart were with me! *My whole heart laughs with joy when I see him.* I offer myself entirely to him.")

Motetus
Deduisant
com fins amourous,
m'en aloie tout pensant;
trois dames trovai parlant

et disant,
que trop sunt envieus
lor mari et trop gaitant.
L'u(n)ne di en sospirant:
"Duel ai trop grant,
quant si au desoz
nos vont nos maris menant;
or voisent bien espiant,
nos les ferons cous;
a leur couz
nos irons jouant.
Dieus les face mourir toz
a no vivant!
S'em proi a genouz:
Pleüst a Diu, que chascune de nous　　　　vdB 1489
tenist la piau de son mari jalouz!"

(Amusing myself like a true lover, I went pensively off. I found three ladies talking and saying that their husbands were terribly jealous and quite watchful. One of them, sighing, said: "I am most sorrowful; our husbands take such a high hand with us—they go around spying on us so much. But we will cuckold them—we will play with their horns! May God make them all die in our lifetime! I beg Him on my knees. *May it please God that each of us have the skin of her jealous husband."*)

In a nutshell, these two texts feature the voices of *malmariées* who are talking among themselves, without filters, about how to pay back their husbands for spying on them and acting out their jealousy. In short, the women cheat on their husbands. Only the first speaker in the triplum suggests she has concerns about pursuing love outside of marriage when she utters refrain vdB 532: "God I dare not go to my sweetheart! How shall I have mercy?"—though it is unclear whether a moral sense or fear of being caught underlies her words. Otherwise, the women defiantly state their decision to engage in extramarital pursuits. In the case of the motetus, there is even an expressed wish that the husbands die, leaving them widows. Once again, the parodic juxtaposition of these overtly adulterous women to the tenor's chaste Virgin, dedicated Bride of Christ, is striking.

In summary, five *malmariée* motets on Assumption tenors survive: two on *VERITATEM* and three on *PORTARE*. Whereas the paschal season motets brought the *malmariée* into dialogue with the tenor messages of Christ's sacrifice, the Assumption motets pit their *malmariée* against the selfless Virgin Mary celebrated in their tenors. The *VERITATEM* chant fragment brings to mind Mary assumed into Heaven to join Christ in a mystical marriage. While the *PORTARE* fragment does not offer so direct a message about Mary as Bride, the context of the Assumption invites a listener to extrapolate from the tenor's words about Mary's early devotion to Christ ("bearing Him") to her heavenly role as His dedicated Bride. As suggested in the above interpretations, motet creators considered both Assumption tenors ripe targets for parodic interplay with the topos of the unhappily married woman. In one case, the *malmariée* voice also contrasts with an upper-voice text in the *grand chant courtois* tradition, adding additional levels of meaning.

In closing, this chapter briefly considers a sixth motet, built on the tenor *VALE* from *Ave regina caelorum*, a Marian antiphon that relates to the Assumption through its shared message and possible historical connection to that liturgy: *Biaus dous amis, quel conseil me donrés?* (776a)/*Grant pechiet fist cis qui m'a mariée* (776b)/*VALE* (O49). The motet is a unicum in Turin, Biblioteca reale, varia 42 (**Tu**), fol. 16. Both upper-voice texts present a monologue by a *malmariée*:

Triplum
Biaus dous amis, queil conseilh me donreis?
De mun marit le dangier ne welh ne ne pui plus endureir,
car sovent le voi cangier de corouch, cant a vos me voit parleir.
Bien sai k'ilh est por vos enjalosi e entreis,
car ilh me soloit sovent rire et mult bellement a parleir,
or le voi si cruelment vers moi soventes fois regardeir
ke je croi, mien esscient,
s'ilh vos plaist, et vos wet agreeir,
ke nos en irons vriement entre mi et vos deporteir,
ou de mun marit, por Dieu, me delivreis.

Motetus
Grant pechiet fist cis ki m'at marieie
cant plus ne puis demoreir avec vos,
biaus dous amis, ke curte demoreie
ki at si tost cornei la matineie:
ne quidoie pas k'encores fuist jours.
Or m'en irai avec cel, or ja l'o,
si li dirai ke ceste demoreie
ai fait anuit avec mes dous secours.
Biaus dous amis, a ceste bien aleie

mi baisereis une fois, et je vos.
Ce poise moi k'a vilain sui doneie
cant je ne puis oblieir mes amurs.[17]

The *malmariée* addresses her lover (*Biaus dous amis*) in both texts: in the triplum, she requests his advice in handling her husband who displays jealousy and a combative nature; in the motetus, she laments that their time together is short, says she will not forget him after she leaves, and again expresses resentment toward her husband (*vilain*).

The tenor chant *VALE* derives from the Marian antiphon *Ave regina celorum ... vale o valde decora et pro nobis Christum exora*. (Hail, O Queen of Heaven ... Fairest thou, where all are fair, Plead with Christ our souls to spare). The four Marian antiphons have been sung at the close of Compline since the thirteenth century, but were not officially assigned to specific liturgical seasons until the sixteenth century. All but one address Mary as Queen of Heaven, and all but one present her as man's heavenly intercessor with Christ (*Ave regina* does both). The antiphons' rhetoric thus aligns them with that of the Assumption Offertory, as discussed above. A tantalizing fact is that Peter Wagner found *Ave regina* assigned to None on the Feast of the Assumption in a twelfth-century Parisian source. Also of note is the grouping of the four antiphons together in antiphoners and processionals with the Proper of the Assumption.[18]

The present motet tenor *VALE* specifically draws attention to Mary's beauty, an attribute that looms large in the Assumption liturgy's incorporation of Psalm 44, as discussed above. Although the upper-voice texts do not play upon that image, their sentiments nevertheless invite an interpretation of the *malmariée* as the antithesis of the devoted Mary of the tenor, who reigns as Christ's Bride in Heaven. Such a parodic treatment aligns this motet with Assumption-related motets discussed in this chapter.

---

17 Text transcribed by Alberto Rizzuti, "Torino 6 unica: Un'indagine preliminare sul manoscritto Varia 42/2 della Biblioteca Reale," *Studi Francesi* 190 (LXIV/1) (2020): 84–112, at 95–96.
18 See Ruth Steiner, "Ave regina caelorum," in https://www.encyclopedia.com/religion/encyclopedias-almanacs-transcripts-and-maps/ave-regina-caelorum.

3 Other Liturgical Tenors

In this chapter I consider three motets suggesting an engagement with the *malmariée* topos that are built on liturgical tenors falling outside of the paschal season or the feast of the Assumption. Of the three, **Mo** 7, 276 directly mentions marriage, whereas **Mo** 6, 212 and **Mo** 2, 30 relate to the *malmariée* topos in a less explicit manner.

The double motet **Mo** 7, 276 [*Nus ne se doit* ...] (601a/922)/[*Je sui en melencolie* ...] (601b/923)/[*AVE VERUM CORPUS*](M84) presents a triplum in which a male thanks Love for making him love such a worthy woman, from whom he must now part, rhetoric that falls squarely within the *grand chant courtois* tradition (emphasis added):

Triplum
[Nus ne se doit ...
...-]gier,
car au mien cuidier,
qui de tout le monde serchier
vorroit chascune partie,
n'i trouveroit mie
si bien afaitie,
et quant Amour me veut prisier,
tant qu'amer me fait **sans folie**
dame si proisie.
Mout dol tel don avoir chier
n'ennuier ne me doit mie,
mes mout l'en doi mercier.
Dame de tous biens garnie,
merci vous requier!
Aidier me voelliés, si com je prie
de cuer sans boisier.
A Dieu, douce amie!

Mon cuer n'emport mie,
ne je ne l'en quier:
O vous le m'estuet laissier.

(No one should ... for, in my opinion, anyone who would search the whole world over, would not find anyone so perfect, and love pays me great honor when he makes me love **without folly** such a worthy lady. I must hold such a gift dear; it should not distress me, rather, I should thank him for it very much. Lady endowed with every fine quality, I beg mercy of you. Deign to help me, I beg you from my heart, without deception. Farewell, sweetheart! I do not take my heart with me, nor do I desire it: I must leave it with you.)

Motetus
[Je sui en melencolie ...]
...-]le talon.
Las, trop s'est de moi eslongie
toute boune compaignie,
qu'onques, puisque mariés fui **sans raison**,
n'ai un seul jour se mal non.
De mener tel vie, compaignon,
envie n'aiés mie;
car **fols** est, qui se marie.

(Melancholy has me ... the heel. Alas! All good company is so far away from me that never, because I **foolishly** married, will I ever have anything but sorrow. My friend, think not favorably on leading such a life: he who marries is **crazy**.)

Its motetus, on the other hand, presents a twist on the unhappily married topos: it features a married *man* lamenting that he foolishly married, lost good company in doing so, and expects never to experience anything but sorrow. He ends somewhat dramatically with "he who marries is crazy." His attack on marriage expresses a view that a man can experience marital discontent because he loses his former way of life. In hearing this text, a listener might reflect non-judgmentally on how both its speaker and the *malmariée* known from the song tradition express negative reactions to marriage. Or, a listener might interpret the man's words as parodic, intended to mock the *malmariée*.

The motet's tenor presents the music of a short Eucharistic chant, *Ave verum corpus*, which highlights Christ's bodily sufferings for mankind, and asks Him to "be for us a foretaste of the heavenly banquet in the trial of death!" The husband's expressed marital suffering perhaps relates allegorically to the tenor's message of Christ's profound trial even unto death. Yet the dramatically contrasting levels of suffering could suggest a parody of the married man's complaints.[1] Another meaning arises when the husband's suffering is heard in dialogue with the triplum male's idealization of love: two males speak, one engaged in a very real-life situation, the other in a distanced, probably unfulfilled love. The motet creator skillfully invites a comparison by tying the two texts together through their highlighted words: the male of the triplum loves *sans folie*, while the male of the motetus married *sans raison* and concludes that one who marries is *fols*. In this play on the concept of foolishness, loving from afar is not madness, but getting married is. In short, the motet casts negative light on the institution of marriage and its complaining participants.

In **Mo** 6, 212, the two-voice *Amis, vostre demoree* (829a)/*DECANTATUR* (whose tenor was misidentified as *Pro patribus* in its only source), *DECANTATUR* is taken from the Office *Gaudeat Hungaria*, sung on the feast day of St. Elizabeth of Hungary (November 17) at Cambrai.[2] *DECANTATUR* derives specifically from the fifth Matins responsory of the Office, *Ante dies exitus*, which depicts Elizabeth joining a bird in song on her deathbed.[3] The melisma accompanying the final syllables "-tatur" of *DECANTATUR* circulated as an independent thirteenth-century motet tenor, specifically in *Amis, vostre demoree*/*DECANTATUR*, but also in another two-voice motet, the hagiographical *Un chant renvoisie* (829b)/*DECANTATUR*, whose upper voice explicitly names and praises Elizabeth. Catherine Bradley has argued that the creator of *Amis, vostre demoree*, in fact, knew the other motet and adopted its tenor, as well as a number of its features.[4]

The motetus text of **Mo** 6, 212 features a woman addressing her lover:

Amis, vostre demoree
me feit d'amours a celee
sentir les dolours;

---

1 Huot would probably interpret this juxtaposition as "allegory used for parodic purposes." *Allegorical Play*, 11.
2 Elizabeth's heart was sent to Cambrai as a relic.
3 Bradley, *Polyphony in Medieval Paris*, Chapter 6: "Intertextuality, Song and Female Voices in Motets on a St Elizabeth of Hungary Tenor," 180, notes the discovery of the origins of the plainchant tenor by Barbara Haggh, *Two Offices for Saint Elizabeth of Hungary: 'Gaudeat Hungaria' and 'Letare Germania,'* ed. Barbara Haagh (Ottawa: Institute of Mediaeval Music, 1995), xv. To date, its status in published catalogues remains "unidentified" and no scholar has assigned it an Office number.
4 Bradley, *Polyphony in Medieval Paris*, 179–211.

car vostres est toz
mes cuers, s'il tant voz agree,
et sera tous jors.
Ne ja, se ce n'est par voz,
n'en voel estre desevree,
puisqu'a vos me sui donee.
Et biax cuers douz,
quant plus me bat et destraint li jalous,   vdB 1555
tant ai ge miex en amor ma pensee.[5]

(Beloved, your absence makes me feel the pain of secret love; for my heart is yours entirely—it if should please you—and always will be. And never unless it is by you do I wish to be parted from it, since I have given myself to you. And fair, sweet heart, *the more the jealous one beats and oppresses me, all the more do I have love in my thoughts.*)

In her interpretation of *Amis, vostre demoree/DECANTATUR*, Bradley reviews the contemporaneous literature on St. Elizabeth that might explain the motetus's use of an ending refrain, vdB 1555, which refers to a "jealous one" beating a woman because she loves someone else. Bradley notes that the refrain also appears as the closing refrain of every verse in a *chanson de femme*, *Amours me fait renvoisier et chanter*, attributed to Moniot d'Arras (fl. 1213–39), in a clear example of a male trouvère adopting a female voice.[6] The woman speaker of the chanson refers to her *ami* in verses 1, 3, and 5 and specifically to "my husband" (*mon mari*) in verse 5, which reads:

Nus ne me doit reprendre ne blasmer
Se j'ai ami, car plevir vous porroie
C'on ne porroit en mon mari trouver
Nule teche dont on amer le doie.
Il me gaite, maiz son tans pis emploie
Que cil qui veut sour gravele semer,
Quar il iert cous, ja n'iere si guardee.
Quant plus me bat et destraint li jalous,
Tant ai je pluz en amours ma pensee.[7]

---

5 I have emended the text and translation in the Mo edition to reflect corrections and improvements that appear in *Songs of the Women Trouvères*, no. 59, p. 202.
6 Observed by Bradley, "Song and Quotation in Two-Voice Motets for Saint Elizabeth of Hungary," *Speculum* 92 (2017), 661–91, at 687.
7 The song text is found in *Chanter m'estuet*, 298–300.

Based on an assumption that the motet creator probably knew Moniot's chanson (an issue discussed further in Chapter 5), Bradley interprets the "jealous one" in the motet text as the speaker's husband, and thus embraces this motet within the *malmariée* topos. She notes that all surviving evidence corroborates that Elizabeth *was* married, but devoted herself to good works only *after* her husband's death. Accordingly, Bradley hesitates to interpret the woman's position in the motet (balanced between her jealous husband and her secret love) as a direct allegory for a conflict on Elizabeth's part between her marital duties and her love of God. But another important fact bears on an interpretation of the motetus, especially its refrain: Elizabeth's spiritual guardian, Master Conrad of Marburg, disciplined her into obedience by encouraging her to flagellate herself and by sanctioning her beatings by others. One writing, *Dicta quatuor ancillarum,* records instances where Elizabeth herself asked to be beaten.[8] Bradley's interpretation in view of these facts is worth quoting in full:

> Unlike Conrad, however, although the husband in the motet beats his wife in order to obstruct her illicit desires, he succeeds, unintentionally, in fueling them. Nevertheless, the refrain's dictum that the more one is beaten the more one loves operates powerfully in the context of the St. Elizabeth tenor. While the refrain's beatings are physical and worldly, its loving is abstract in thought, just as Elizabeth's bodily mortifications served the purpose of bringing her closer to God in prayer and soul.[9]

Bradley thus argues for an allegorical reading: The beatings by a presumably jealous husband in the motet text relate to the beatings Elizabeth endured in her own life, both of which fuel the punished individual's love: in the case of the wife of the motetus, resolutely for another man; in Elizabeth's case, submissively for God. Given the contrasting results, the motet may also have invited a parodic reading that mocks the unfaithful wife.[10]

Mo 2, 30, the four-voice *Cest quadruble sans reison* (798)/*Voz n'i dormirés ja mais* (799)/*Biaus cuers renvoisiés et douz* (800)/*FIAT*, is associated with the Holy Trinity Saturday Vespers through its tenor *FIAT* taken from the responsory text (O54): *Benedictus dominus. Replebitur*

---

[8] Bradley, *Polyphony in Medieval Paris,* 205.
[9] Ibid.
[10] This may be an instance of what Huot calls "allegory used for parodic purposes" (*Allegorical Play,* 11).

majestate eius omnia terra fiat. (Blessed be his glorious name for ever: and let the whole earth be filled with his glory).[11] The feast of the Holy Trinity is celebrated one week after Pentecost, the official end of Paschal Tide. Whereas **Mo** 6, 212 linked to the *malmariée* topos through its mention of a "jealous" one, whom a listener might have associated with the jealous husband of a *chanson de femme* that shares its refrain, **Mo** 2, 30 may have triggered reflections on a *malmariée* only in a more roundabout manner. We begin with an examination of the motet's female-voiced triplum (emphasis added), which Anna Grau calls a *chanson de malmariée*.[12]

Triplum
line 1   *Voz n'i dormirés ja mais,*   vdB 1867
line 2   **vilains** tres chetis et la[i]s;
         vostre acoi[n]tance
         m'est trop a grevance:
         Trop avés depleit.
         N'aim pas vo samblance,
         si n'en puis je mes;
         las, quant je fui en vos las
         et je gisoie entre vos bras,
         dolans, n'i feites [n'es] as.
         Tenes vous en pais;
line 12   *fi! quar trop vous trovai ma[u]vés*   vdB 1867
line 13   *au premier solas.*

(*You will never sleep there*, you dastardly, miserable **scoundrel**; knowing you grieve me immeasurably: you have greatly displeased me. I can't stand your looks—I can't take it anymore; alas, when I was caught in your trap and lay mournfully within your arms, you didn't do anything at all. Keep quiet! *Fie! for I found you exceedingly bad from the first embrace.*)

vdB 1867 appears in *L'Art d'amours*, a vernacular translation of Ovid's *Ars amatoria*, supplemented with lengthy interpretive glosses that include many refrains. vdB 1867 appears near the end of Book 2, which, along with Book 1, was written after 1214–15, but within the

---

11 See van der Werf, *Integrated Directory*, 133–34, for the labeling of the responsory as O54.
12 Grau, "Representation and Resistance," Figure 5.1 and pp. 165–66.

first third of the thirteenth century.[13] Given the dating of **Mo** fascicle 2 to the late 1270s or 1280s,[14] the creator of this motet could well have known the refrain from the *L'Art d'amours*.

The immediate context for the refrain in *L'Art d'amours* does not clearly implicate a married woman as the speaker. The refrain falls within a gloss of this statement in Ovid's text: "I said that if you want to have good pleasure with love, take a woman of good age who is not too young" (lines 3484–85). The gloss presents a dialogue between a male lover and a woman, quoted here in its entirety (emphasis added):

The lover talks about the desire of the pleasure of which he speaks here in this song of regret:
 "*Beautiful, happy and sweet heart,*   vdB 217
 When will I sleep with you,
 In your beautiful arms?"

Because he had not served her well to her liking, she answered him:
 "*You will never sleep here:*   vdB 1867
 You have found too much bad
 And too little good pleasure!"

Because he had not served her well, she did not keep herself from saying firmly to him that he would never sleep there. Therefore, she calls him a **peasant** [*vilain*] and says to him:
 "These are not arms for a **peasant** to sleep with,
 I will never sleep in your arms." (lines 3486–98)[15]

Throughout his treatise, Ovid probably intended his advice on love to apply to married as well as unmarried men and women, which we get an inkling of when he states in the slightly earlier lines 3455–62 that some women view [sexual] "play" only as a housewife's duty, a viewpoint he frowns upon. In the specific gloss under discussion, the word *vilain* might trigger thoughts of an unhappily married woman, because

---

13 See Introduction, note 12.
14 *Grove Music Online*, "Sources, MS," offers summary dating for fascs. 2–6, the "old corpus": "1270s (Rosketh and *RISM*, c1280)." In the "Introduction" to *The Montpellier Codex: The Final Fascicle*, ed. Catherine A. Bradley and Karen Desmond (Woodbridge and Rochester, NY: Boydell Press, 2018), 1, the editors offer a slightly more delimited dating of the "old corpus," the late 1270s or 1280s, which is adopted in the present study. In "The Compilation of the Montpellier Codex," *Early Music History* 11 (1992): 263–301, at 300, Mary E. Wolinski posits a controversial view that fascs. 1–7 were copied as an entity in the 1260s or 1270s.
15 Translation by Blonquist, *L'Art d'amours*, 118.

it is often applied by a wife to her husband in the *malmariée* corpus of songs and motets and in fabliaux. Certainly, the thirteenth-century individual who glossed Ovid's text could have been familiar with these literary contexts, as well as the word's more general meaning as a person of uncouth mind and matters, often associated with a member of a lower social class (the gloss translation uses "peasant"). Importantly, at a time when arranged marriages were still current, impoverished women of lower nobility engaged in interclass marriage with wealthy peasants because of economic necessity. Nonetheless, as Kathryn Gravdal argues, shifting boundaries between social classes became a preoccupation of legal and literary contexts in the time under consideration. Accordingly, a text's use of *vilian* and *courtois* does not necessarily denote a simple binary class distinction. Gravdal refers by way of example to the epic *Gaydon*, in which "a *courtois* chooses to become a *vilain* and exalts the advantages of that life. Gaydon makes a clear distinction between the social and moral meanings of the term: 'Cil est vilains qui fait la vilennie'."[16]

Returning to the four-part motet, its connection to the *L'Art d'amours* gloss is clear. Its triplum appropriates the woman's first three-line statement (vdB 1867), dividing it to become a framing device—see lines 1 and 12–13 in the triplum text given above—with line 2 introducing the word *vilain* found in the gloss commentary. With respect to the other upper-voice texts, the fact that the quadruplum and motetus are spoken by a male in contrast to the female-voice triplum is not extraordinary in and of itself, but, importantly, the male-voice motetus uses vdB 217, the opening words spoken by the male in the give-and-take between male and female in the same *L'Art d'amours* gloss:

Motetus
line 1   *Biaus cuers renvoisiés et douz,*   vdB 217
         tuit me deduit sunt en voz;
         or ne m'est il riens d'autrui dangier,
         quant je de tot Angiers
         aim la plus senee,
         qui mieus pleist a toz.
         Douce desirree,
         sans fiel et sanz gas,
         pleine de solas,

---

16 Kathryn Gravdal, *Vilain and Courtois: Transgressive Parody in French Literature of the Twelfth and Thirteenth Centuries* (Lincoln: University of Nebraska Press, 1989), 14.

50 Malmariée *Motets in Relationship to Their Tenors*

	biauté tres bien nee,	
	taille(e) a compas,	
	hé, doz Dieus,	
line 13	quant dormirai j'avec vous,	vdB 217
line 14	entre voz dous bras?	

(*Cheerful, fair, sweet heart*, all of my pleasure comes from you now. I have need of nothing from anyone else since I love the wisest lady in all of Angers, this one whom everyone finds the most pleasing. Sweet beloved, void of malice and of derision, full of comfort, high-born beauty, sculpted to perfection, oh, sweet God, *when will I sleep with you, sleep in your sweet arms?*)

As was true in the triplum, the motetus uses its three-line refrain from *L'Art d'amours* as a frame (lines 1 and 13–14). In effect, the dialogue between male and female found in the *L'Art d'amours* has been transformed into simultaneous utterances by two voices of the four-voice motet, with their respective refrains sounding against one another.

In discussing this motet, Sylvia Huot does not connect the motet texts with the *L'Art d'amours*, but recognizes the interconnected nature of the motet texts themselves: she views the woman's words as an apparent response to the question posed by the man in the motetus. She believes that the male-voiced quadruplum "issues a further declaration of love on the part of the man." Though Huot refers to the woman as "rejecting a suitor" in the manner of the shepherdess of the *pastourelle*, who engages the suitor in debate, she also says that a second possible analogy for the motet is the *chanson de malmariée* in which "a woman rejects the sexual attentions of her husband, often expressing her preference for a more attractive, more virile lover." In either case, for Huot, the context of a debate looms large.[17]

A final question concerns the role of the tenor *FIAT*, whose Psalm 72 source praises the Israelite king as an instrument of divine justice, a representative of God. An interpretation of the triplum and motetus in relationship to the tenor does not come immediately to mind. But a tenor resonance does arise when we consider the concordant double

---

17 Sylvia Huot, "Polyphonic Poetry: The Old French Motet and its Literary Context," *French Forum* 14 (1989), 261–78, at 262–64. Huot refers to lyric insertions within narrative texts to add color to amorous dialogue and debate. For example, in the *Roman de la Violette* "Euriaut sings the first stanza of a *chanson de mal mariée*, adapting the rejection of the jealous husband to fit that of the would-be suitor" (Ibid., 264).

Latin motet in Bamberg, Staatsbibliothek, Lit. 115 (**Ba**), no. 3, fol. 2v, *Ave, virgo regia/Ave, plena gracie/FIAT*, whose triplum, motetus, and tenor music match that of **Mo** 2, 30. Its triplum in particular relates Mary to the tenor's message of divine justice: *Tu, mater regis, tu obscura legis glosas omnia; deviantes regis per hec invia propria clemencia* (Thou mother of the king, thou dost make clear all the obscurities of the Law; thou rulest those wandering through life's difficulties, with thy special mercy). In effect, Mary arbitrates in matters of justice through her God-given mercy. Based on the corresponding message of the tenor and upper-voice texts in **Ba**, one can reasonably conclude that it preceded the composition of **Mo** 2, 30, where such a close relationship is not immediately evident. The long-standing dating of **Ba** to 1275 allows that its version could predate that of **Mo** 2, 30.[18] The latter would then have created a French contrafact version of the Latin double motet, to which it added a quadruplum voice, whose text is as follows:

Quadruplum
Cest quadruble sans reison
n'ai pas fete en tel seison,
qu'oisel chanter n'ose.
Quar se je repose
de fere chançon,
s'amor, qui arose
mon cuer environ,
ne perdra grant souprison.
Se ai esté lonc tens
en sa prison
et en atent guerredon,
biaus sui de sens:
Quant si bele dame m'aime,   vdB 1540
Je ne demant plus.

(I didn't compose this quadruplum with no reason at all in a season during which even birds dare not sing. For if I leave off composing songs, Love, who nourishes my heart, will not lose a thing of value.

---

18 See Karl-Georg Pfändtne, "Zum Enstehungsraum der Bamberger Motettenhandschrift Msc. Lit. 115 – kodikologische und kunsthistorische Argumente," *Acta musicologica* 84 (2012): 161–66, for consideration of provenance and dating.

I have been long in this prison and await recompense; I am in my right senses: *when such a fair lady loves me, I ask for nothing more*.)

Did the creator of **Mo** 2, 30 intend the quadruplum to convey a message in relationship to the tenor? Jennifer Saltzstein suggests that is the case, stating that the tenor's "jubilant, celebratory character" is "aligned with the subject of the fourth voice of this motet."[19] She argues that the quadruplum speaker privileges his mastery of the conventions of song composition over the anguished suffering typically experienced by male lovers, and, in so doing, valorizes his own authorial role.[20] But she does not explicitly connect the valorization back to the tenor *FIAT*. This quadruplum text undoubtedly depicts a male who cherishes love's role in his life, a sentiment difficult to relate to the tenor's exaltation of a king who rules justly in the name of God. Thus, it appears that none of **Mo** 2, 30's upper-voice texts intersect with the tenor message, which can be explained by its contrafact status. In Chapter 6 I explore upper-voice readings that emerge when the quadruplum refrain vdB 1540 is considered within an intertextual nexus of motets. In the meantime, **Mo** 2, 30 fits into the present study because thirteenth-century listeners may have heard *malmariée* resonances within its language, even if not as readily as is the case with many other examples in this corpus.

In summary, three motets on Latin tenors that fall outside of the paschal and Assumption liturgies engage with the *malmariée* topos in individual ways. **Mo** 6, 212, based on a tenor from the liturgy of St. Elizabeth of Hungary, seems to connect beatings she experienced at the hand of her spiritual guardian Conrad with a wife's beatings in the *chanson de femme* with which it shares its refrain. An indirect allegory may be at play, but because the beatings lead to differing experiences of love—religious adherence versus marital infidelity, this juxtaposition may have been viewed as a parody of the unfaithful wife. **Mo** 7, 276 stands apart because it presents the voice of an unhappily married man rather than a woman, perhaps inducing reflections on how both genders can experience discontent in marriage, or mocking the usually complaining *malmariée*. The male's suffering resonates with that of Christ encapsulated in its Eucharistic tenor, perhaps allegorically and parodically. The foolishness of his decision to marry is intensified by

---

[19] Jennifer Saltzstein, *The Refrain and the Rise of the Vernacular in Medieval French Music and Poetry*, Gallica 30 (Woodbridge and Rochester, NY: D. S. Brewer, 2013), 64. See pp. 59–69 for her full discussion of the motet. Page 65 includes another translation of the quaduplum.

[20] Ibid., 66–67.

its comparison with the seemingly blissful state of mind projected by the motet's other male, who basks in his idealized love. The message is clear: men too could regret marriage. Finally, **Mo** 2, 30 stands in the least direct relationship to its tenor, which praises God as an instrument of divine justice, because of its apparent status as a contrafact. It is included in the *malmariée* motet corpus here because it incorporates refrains from *L'art d'amours* in a debate format, where the female speaker might be a married woman.

4 French Tenors and French Text Only

In this chapter I discuss four remaining *malmariée* motets that stand apart from the fourteen with liturgical Latin tenors: two with French tenors (**Mo** 7, 271 and **Mo** 8, 325) and two that survive with only an upper-voice French text (EM 389 and 415). Although these *malmariée* texts do not enter into dialogue with a liturgical tenor, they offer a view of a woman's reactions to marital realities in the thirteenth century, and of how her opinions on love contrast with those of males in other voices.

Mo 7, 271, *Dame bele et avenant et de biau port* (872)/*Fi, mari, de vostre amour!* (873)/*NUS N'IERT JA JOLIS, S'IL N'AIME*, is built on a tenor in the form of a French rondeau:

Tenor
Nus n'iert ja jolis,   vbB 1407
s'il n'aime!
[Dame de haut pris,
(nus n'iert ja jolis,)
li vostres amis
vous claime:
Nus n'iert ja jolis,
s'il n'aime!]

(*No one will ever be happy unless he loves*: [Lady of great renown (*no one will ever be happy*), your sweetheart calls to you! *No one will ever be happy unless he loves.*])

Like the tenor, the triplum features a male voice addressing an exalted lady in the tradition of the *grand chant courtois*:

Triplum
Dame bele et avenant et de biau port,

DOI: 10.4324/9781003335405-6

arrivé sui a mal port:
Je muir a grant tort.
Se je n'ai de vous comfort,
sans nul resort
sui mis a la mort.

(Beautiful lady, worthy and good, I have come to an evil end: I am dying so unfairly. If I have no comfort from you, there is no recourse: I am put to death.)

Simultaneously, the married woman of the motetus addresses her husband with defiance:

Motetus

Fi, mari, de vostre amour!	vdB 746
Quar j'ai aimi,	
tel com il afiert a mi,	
qui me sert et nuit et jour	
sanz sejour	
de cuer mignot et joli.	
Vilains, vous demorés	vdB 1842
et je m'en vois a li!	

(*Fie on your love, husband! For I have a lover* that is suitable for me; he serves me night and day, without respite, and with a joyful, affectionate heart. *Wretch, you will stay here, and I will go to him!*)

The *malmariée* tells her husband directly about being served night and day by her lover. Her satisfying, *consummated* love outside of marriage contrasts with the triplum male's unrequited love that "kills him," expressed in the pained rhetoric of the *grand chant courtois*. At the same time, the *malmariée* seems to respond to the dictum offered by the tenor's male speaker: "No one will ever be happy unless he loves." Whereas that male appeals futilely to the *Dame de haut pris* to grant him love, the *malmariée* finds a willing lover and acts. Thus, in both cases, she parodies the aristocratic model of love in which a male waits for love.

Mo 8, 325, *S'on me regarde, s'on me regarde* (908)/*Prennés i garde, s'on me regarde* (909)/*HÉ MI ENFANT*, is a second *malmariée* motet built on a French tenor. Like **Mo** 7, 271, its tenor unfolds as a rondeau.[1]

---

[1] See Mark Everist, "Motets, French Tenors, and the Polyphonic Chanson ca. 1300," *The Journal of Musicology* 24 (2007): 365–406, at 392, where he refers to an irregular six-line rondeau, which may be a borrowed monophonic song.

Anna Grau refers to both of the upper-voice texts as *chansons de malmariées* in her Table 1. She claims the motet "clearly refers to the tradition of the *carole*: a queen of the dance leads a group of young lovers who rebel against jealous husbands and other nay-sayers" and "both voices denounce the interference of jealous outsiders; the female subject seems to address her remarks to companions and refers to her immediate surroundings, suggesting that she is in a particular social setting."[2] Its upper-voice texts are given here in full:

Triplum

S'on me regarde,   vdB 1531
s'on me regarde,
dites le moi;
trop sui gaillarde,
bien l'aperchoi.
Ne puis laissier, que mon
regard ne s'esparde,
car tes m'esgarde,
dont mout me tarde,
qu'il m'ait o[u] soi,
qu'il a en foi
de m'amour plain otroi.
Mais tel ci voi,
qui est, je croi,
(feu d'enfer l'arde!)
jalous de moi.
Mais pour li d'amer ne recroi,
car par ma foi
pour nient m'esgarde,
bien pert sa garde:
J'arai rechoi!

(*If anyone looks at me, if anyone looks at me, tell me*. I see well that I am too daring; I can't stop my eyes from wandering, for when a certain one looks at me, I can hardly wait for him to have me with him and receive in faith the gift of my love in full measure. But I see another here who is, I believe (may hell fire burn him!), jealous of me. But I refuse to

---

2 Grau, "Representation and Resistance," with quotations on pp. 193–94 and 195, respectively.

cease loving on his account, for by my faith it doesn't do him any good to watch me; he's wasting his time: I'll find an escape!)

Motetus
Prennés i garde,   vdB 1531
s'on me regarde;
trop sui gaillarde,
dites le moi,
pour Dieu vous proi.
Car tes m'esgarde,
dont mout me tarde,
qu'il m'ait o[u] soi,
bien l'aperchoi;
et tel chi voi,
qui est, je croi,
(feu d'enfer larde!)
jalous de moi.
Mais pour li d'amer ne recroi,
pour nient m'esgarde,
bien pert sa garde:
J'arai rechoi
et do mon ami le dosnoi!
Faire le doi,
ne serai plus couarde.

(*Take note if anyone looks at me; I am too daring, so tell me*, in the name of God, I beg you. For when one looks at me, I can hardly wait for him to have me with him. And I see another here who is, I believe (may hell fire burn him!), jealous of me. But I refuse to cease loving on his account; it doesn't do him any good to watch me, he's wasting his time: I'll find an escape and have the love of my sweetheart. I must do it; I will be a coward no longer.)

Though Grau claims that the environment suggested by the paired texts is a *carole*, evidence to that effect is lacking. They reveal a female speaker who acknowledges an individual "jealous of me," as well as her determination (1) to escape that person's attempt at control and (2) be with her sweetheart. These expressions open the possibility that the speaker could well be a married woman, but lacking reference to a husband per se, we have to allow that she could be unmarried, pursued by two men, one of whom is jealous.³ This study retains **Mo** 8, 325 in the *malmariée* corpus, despite the unclear marital status of the woman speaker. We return in Chapter 5 to another interpretive layer that derives from the intertextual context of the motet's refrain, vdB 1531.

The *malmariée* corpus also includes two motets that survive with one French text, but no tenor, EM 389, *Osteis lou moi* (1100), and 415, *Trop sui jonette, maris* (1124). They appear in a chansonnier within Oxford, Bodlein Library, **Douce 308**, a source that consists of five individual books, probably produced in the early fourteenth century in Metz in the Lorraine region of northeastern France.⁴ The chansonnier consists of 512 lyrics, and was never intended to contain musical notation. It groups works under generic headings, with the two *malmariée* motets falling within its section labeled "motets and rondeaux."⁵

The woman in EM 389 protests a seemingly arranged marriage, signaled by her final line, "This marriage is not right," part of the split refrain vdB 1463:

Osteis lou moi,	*Take it off,*
L'anelet dou doi!	*This ring on my finger!*
Avoir pas vilains ne me doit,	A boor should not have me,
Car, bien sai, cous en seroit	For I knew well he would end up a cuckold
S'avocke moi	If he were with me
Longement estoit;	For long;
Departir m'an vuel orandroit,	I want to leave him right now,
Je ne suix pas mariee a droit.	This marriage is not right.⁶

---

3 Ibid. Grau seems to acknowledge the unmarried possibility when she refers to "jealous outsiders."

4 In *The Old French Ballette: Oxford, Bodleian Library, MS Douce 308*, ed., trans., and intro. Egal Doss-Quinby and Samuel N. Rosenberg; music editions and commentary by Elizabeth Aubrey (Geneva: Droz, 2006), xlvi, the editors state, "probably produced in Metz in the first decade of the fourteenth century." Sylvia Huot, in *From Song to Book: The Poetics of Writing in Old French Lyric and Lyrical Narrative Poetry* (Ithaca, NY: Cornell University Press, 1987), 170, refers to **Douce 308** as copied in Metz during the first half of the fourteenth century.

5 Mary Atchison discusses the makeup of the manuscript in *The Chansonnier of Oxford Bodleian MS Douce 308: Essays and Complete Edition of Texts* (Aldershot and Burlington, VT: Ashgate, 2005), with particular attention to the motet and rondeaux section on pp. 80–88.

6 Text and translation found in Songs of the *Women Trouvères*, 249–50.

The woman states that she in fact married knowing that she would make her husband a cuckold. She thereby suggests that she was forced to consent to this marriage, and did so without any expectation that she would find personal satisfaction within it. One can imagine that a listener could respond to her discontent with sympathy, mockery, or both.

EM 415 records another married woman's direct speech, with a focus on her unwise marriage to an older man:

Trop suis jonette, maris	I am too young for you, husband
Por vos; trop fut anfantis	It was too foolish
K'il nos fist assambleir	To join us together
Car je ne poroie	For I could not
Teil vie meneir,	Lead such a life,
Ne si ne savroie	Nor could I
Ma joie oblïeier,	Forget my joy,
Ce seroit enfance,	That would be foolish,
Et si ne m'an sai	So I do not know
Coment deporteir:	How to behave:
S'an suis en doutance,	I am in doubt,
En dotance.	In doubt.[7]

Unlike the woman in EM 389, this young wife indicates that she consented to marry an older man naively, thinking that it could work out. Now she faces the realization that she cannot remain in a loveless marriage nor forget having experienced joy before, which may refer to an experience of love, or perhaps to a freer life more generally. She admits she doesn't know how to behave, suggesting a moral sense that contrasts with the impetuosity of other *malmariées* who head straight into adultery or fantasize about doing so.

In summary, two motets on French tenors engage the *malmariée* topos: the motetus in **Mo** 7, 271 parodies the distant, unconsummated love revealed in the triplum and attributes to the *malmariée* agency to experience true love. **Mo** 8, 325 features a woman who wants to get away from a "jealous" one and go to her lover, without specifying whether the woman is married. In EM 389 and 415, transmitted without tenors, the unhappily married woman speaks directly about her arranged marriage, either embracing infidelity without hesitation or revealing uncertainty about how to proceed in a loveless marriage.

[7] Ibid., 250.

Part II
Malmariée Motet Refrains within an Intertextual Nexus

Part I's discussion about treatment of the *malmariée* topos in the motet repertory occasionally touched on matters of transmission, to which I now turn in detail, considering the dating and provenance of each motet's sources, and of the refrain(s) it shares with other genres and other motets. This combined information (1) illuminates the dating and locations for collecting and cultivating *malmariée* motets in the thirteenth century, and (2) provides insight into the flow of popular refrains within a broad swath of literary and musical genres and within the motet corpus itself. Furthermore, I offer an interpretation of how a refrain's meaning may change in bold or subtle ways as a motet creator incorporates it into a new context, often involving intergeneric play, with or without a shift in the gender of the speaking voice.

As shown by the "concordances" column of Table 1, French-texted *malmariée* motets tend to be newly composed or possibly *contrafacta* of Latin motets. Two motets relate to a clausula, but the motet likely preceded the clausula version. The clausula for **Mo 6, 243** appears in Paris, BnF lat. 15139, from Saint-Victor (**StV**), with the motetus text incipit inscribed at its beginning. The scholarly consensus holds that the clausulae in **StV** with accompanying vernacular motet incipits in fact represented motet transcriptions.[1] For **Mo 6, 180**, Gaël

---

1 See Fred Büttner, ed. *Die Klauseln der Handschrift Saint-Victor (Paris, BN, lat. 15139)* (Tutzing: Schneider, 1999); and *Das Klauselrepertoire der Handschrift Saint-Victor (Paris, BN, lat. 15139): Eine Studie zur mehrstimmigen Komposition im 13. Jahrhundert* (Lecce: Milella, 2011). He specifically discusses the relationship between the **StV** clausula and the motet version of **Mo 6, 243** in *Die Klauseln*, 255–61 and 323, and *Das Klauselrepertoire*, 366–70. Bradley, *Polyphony in Medieval Paris*, 81–84, summarizes scholarly debates in the twentieth century on the relationship between clausulae and motets and argues for accepting multi-directionality in thirteenth-century chronologies.

DOI: 10.4324/9781003335405-7

Saint-Cricq discovered that a related clausula appears in **F**, no. 452 (fol. 184r); Catherine Bradley has suggested that this clausula is also a transcribed motet.[2] Fourteen of the eighteen motets in question are found in **Mo**.[3] Table 1's "Concordances" column and the adjacent "Links to other motets through refrains" support a speculation that **Mo** and motet sources **W2** and **N(mo)** participated in a transmission nexus, to be discussed below.

Chapters 5 and 6 present summary tables of all known sources of a refrain that appears within a given malmariée motet: eight motets figure in Chapter 5 (refrain shared with another genre) and five in Chapter 6 (refrain shared with another motet). Two additional malmariée motets that contain refrains are not included because they exhibit no intertextuality.[4] The tables are organized with refrain numbers (vdB) across the top row, and manuscript sources appear in columns, grouped according to whether they transmit the refrain in a motet, a chanson, or "other," a category that includes romances, narrative poems, and treatises. Two sources, Paris, Bibliothèque nationale de France, fr.12615 ("Noailles chansonnier") and Paris, Bibliothèque nationale de France, fr. 844 ("Manuscrit du Roi"), appear in the motet grouping as **N(mo)** and **R(mo)** and in the chanson grouping as **T** and **M**, because they transmit both genres, whose sources were cataloged independently of one another.

---

2 The concordance for **Mo 6** 180 was discovered by Gaël Saint-Cricq; see his "Formes types dans le motet du xiiie siècle: Étude d'un processus répétitif," 2 vols. (Ph.D. diss., University of Southampton, 2009), 1:146. Bradley, "Contrafacta and Transcribed Motets: Vernacular Influences on Latin Motets and Clausulae in the Florence Manuscript," *Early Music History* 32 (2013): 1–70, at 68, n. 179.

3 Of the four *malmariée* motets that do not appear in **Mo**, EM 310 is transmitted in motet sources **N(mo)** and **R(mo)**, EM 389 and 415 are found only in **Douce 308**, and **Tu**, f. 16 is likewise a unicum.

4 EM 415 contains vdB 1818, and **Mo 6**, 243, vdB 1514. Three *malmariée* motets do not transmit refrains: **Mo** 5, 156, **Mo** 7, 276, and **Tu**, f. 16.

5 Motet Refrains Shared with Other Genres

A survey of the sources of the refrains contained in all the *malmariée* motets reveals numerous instances in which the motets share refrains with songs, romances, narrative poems, and treatises, to the exclusion of other motets. Into this category fall eight motets: two early motets (EM 310 and 389); Mo 5, 169; three from **Mo** 6 (180, 203, 212); **Mo** 7, 271; and **Mo** 8, 325. Appendix A, Table 2, summarizes, left to right, refrain data for the EM motets and those in **Mo** 5, 6, and 8. **Mo** 7, 271 is treated separately in Table 3.

With a Song and a Romance or Narrative Poem

EM 310, EM 389, **Mo** 7, 271, and **Mo** 8, 325 fall into this subgroup. In addition to examining specific songs as the possible sources of their refrains, the following analyses also consider the narratives *Roman de la Violette*, *Court d'amours*, and *Renart le Nouvel*, which transmit the relevant refrains within their depictions of aristocratic evenings of song and dance; and *La Court de Paradis*, a narrative poem about a *carole* performed before the Queen of Heaven.

EM 310 *Ja ne mi marierai/AMORIS* is the only one of the four motets in this category that is transmitted with a liturgical tenor. It survives in motet MS **R(mo)** (copied after 1253, probably 1260s or 1270s in Artois, possibly in Arras) and motet MS **N(mo)** (probably copied ca. 1270s in Artois, with a likely connection to Arras). MS **N(mo)** shares its highest motet concordance with MS **R(mo)**, with twenty-five of their shared motets unknown elsewhere. EM 310 is one of their shared motets, without concordances in central sources **F**, **W2**, **Mo**, **MüA**, **Ba**, and **Cl**. Whereas its refrain vdB 1374 *Ne vos mariez mie, tenez vous ensi* is found only in the motet, vdB 1006 *Ja ne mi marierai, més par amors amerai* appears in a number of sources, including a romance *Le Roman de la Violette* or *Géraud de Nevers*, written by Gerbert de Montreuil in the

DOI: 10.4324/9781003335405-8

early thirteenth century, with conjectured dating from 1204 through 1228.[1] *Violette*'s earliest surviving manuscript, **Pa 1374**, was probably copied ca. 1240.[2]

This romance depicts the conventions of a courtly setting, particularly in the matter of love intrigues.[3] Like the *Roman de la rose*, it includes song performance in the course of its storytelling, creating in both cases what Ardis Butterfield calls a *roman à chansons*, in effect a proto-chansonnier.[4] Aside from its quotation of entire song verses (with refrain), *Violette* presents twenty-seven separate refrains, of which sixteen appear only here.[5]

vdB 1006 falls into the group of five refrains in *Roman de la Violette* that also appear in a motet and a chanson, in this case a *chanson avec des refrains* entitled *Chançon veul faire de moi* by trouvère Perrin d'Angicourt (fl. 1245–70), who had a close association with Arras.[6] The chanson is transmitted without music in six trouvère sources: **KN(trv)PX** (all copied 1270–80 in the Picardy-Artois region, with **X** probably from Arras),[7] **V** (after 1266, Artois), and **C** (1290–1300, from Metz in the Lorraine area of northeastern France).[8] The chanson's final strophe presents a woman privileging love over marriage, ending with vdB 1006:

---

1 Dating as given in Saltzstein, *The Refrain and the Rise of the Vernacular*, 14. The romance has been edited by Douglas Labaree Buffum, *Le Roman de la Violette ou de Gerart de Nevers par Gerbert de Montreuil* (Paris: H. Champion, 1928).
2 Ardis Butterfield, *Poetry and Music in Medieval France from Jean Renart to Guillaume de Machaut* (Cambridge: Cambridge University Press, 2002), 26, refers to Buffum's dating of the manuscript as "before 1250" on pp. vii–ix), but she uses "c. 1240" on p. 30.
3 It tells the tale of Euriaut, whom a slanderer falsely accuses of being unfaithful to the man she loves, Gérard. In the course of the romance, Euriaut outsmarts the slanderer and in the end she and Gérard marry. Kristin L. Burr, "Recreating the Body: Euriaut's Tales in *Le Roman de la Violette*," *Symposium* 56/1 (Spring 2002): 3–16, at 3–4 *et passim*.
4 Butterfield, *Poetry and Music*, 27.
5 Of the remaining eleven refrains, three are also transmitted in a chanson, five in a chanson and a motet, two in a chanson and in another romance, and one in a wide array of sources, including a *pastourelle avec des refrains*, a motet, and several treatises. This data compiled by the author of this study is based on the online *Refrain* site.
6 See Theodore Karp, "Perrin d'Angicourt," in *Grove Music Online*.
7 Regarding this manuscript grouping, see Hans G. Spanke, ed., *Eine altfranzösische Liedersammlung: Der anonyme Teil der Liederhandschriften K N P X* (Halle: Max Niemeyer, 1925).
8 For **V**, see Nicholas W. Bleisch, "The Copying and Collection of Music in the Trouvère Chansonnier F-Pn fr. 24406" (Ph.D. diss.: King's College, University of Cambridge, 2018). For **C**, see Cristopher Callahan, "Collecting Trouvère Lyric at the Peripheries: The Lessons of MSS Paris, BnF fr. 20050 and Bern, Burgerbibliothek 389," *Textual Cultures* 8/2 (Fall 2013): 15–30, at 16 and 23–25.

J'ai et amerai touz dis
celui qui m'agree.
Ja, pour nul de mes amis,
n'iere mariee,
se je n'ai prochainement
celui cui j'aim loiaument
. . . .
Ançois la mort atendrai
Ja ne mi marierai   vdB 1006
mais par amours amerai![9]

Because Perrin d'Angicourt flourished *after* the date of *Violette*'s composition, he could have drawn the refrain from an early source of *Violette*, such as **Pa 1374**. Within *Violette*'s scene that depicts a *carole* after a courtly dinner, a number of women sing refrains,[10] with the sister of the count de Blois presenting vdB 1006, and other noble women additional refrains that likewise communicate the idea of favoring love over marriage. That Perrin may have appropriated a refrain from this scene in *Violette* for his chanson verse seems plausible.[11]

As to the motet, the dating and Artesian provenance of its two surviving sources **R(mo)** and **N(mo)** allow that the motet creator could have known the refrain text from the chanson (transmitted in sources from the Picardy-Artois region) or possibly *Violette*. Though no refrain melody survives outside of the motet, the motet creator may nevertheless have been familiar with a refrain melody from the

---

9 Text as given in G. Steffens, ed., *Die Lieder des Troveors Perrin von Angincourt* (Halle: Max Niemeyer, 1905), 250.

10 See discussion by Butterfield, *Poetry and Music*, 50–57, about refrains existing apart from *rondets de carole*, with a particular comparison between refrain usage in the *Roman de la rose* and the *Roman de la Violette*.

11 The *malmariée* topos arises in another song within *Violette*. Anna Grau notes that the romance introduces Euriaut by having her sing a song in her first appearance; in one manuscript, that song is in fact a varied version of the first verse of a *malmariée* chanson by Moniot d'Arras, *Amors mi fait renvoisier et chanter*, though Euriaut is not married at the time. (This is the chanson that shares vdB 1555 with **Mo** 6, 212, but *Violette*'s variant version does not include the refrain.) Grau argues that "following Euriaut's performance of the *chanson de malmariée*, however, the narrative adapts to the situation described in the lyric: the slanderer uses deception to paint Euriaut as an unfaithful wife and force Gerart into the role of jealous and violent 'husband.'" Grau, "Representing 'Women's Songs' in Stories: Lyric Interpolations and Female Characters in *Guillaume de Dole* and the *Roman de la Violette*," *Essays in Medieval Studies* 27 (2011), 33–44, at 40.

chanson tradition, or composed it from scratch.[12] As discussed in Chapter 1, the motet sets this refrain that privileges love over marriage against the Pentecostal tenor *AMORIS*, which expresses a wish for divine love conveyed through the Holy Spirit. In the motet context, one can interpret the woman's statement as allegorizing the tenor, i.e. she intends to devote herself to a spiritual instead of an earthly love. Or it can be read as parodying the tenor, either on its own or through its recall of the woman's flippant tone in the chanson and *Violette*.

EM 389 *Osteis lou moi*, transmitted without a tenor, is one of two *malmariée* motets that survive in a chansonnier within **Douce 308**, a source probably produced in the early fourteenth century in Metz. The chansonnier is copied by the same two scribes who penned the manuscript's adjacent *Tournoi de Chauvency*, composed in 1285. The shared aspects of script and contents (e.g. certain refrains, named individuals, and mention of a *robardel*) suggest that these two parts of **Douce 308** were "of one conception and therefore constitute a medieval compilation."[13] This compilation depicts conventions of the aristocratic world, with the *Tournoi* focused on people assembling for a series of tournaments, followed by evenings of song and dance that include the singing of refrains.[14] In both its depiction of aristocratic conventions and its repertory of refrains, the *Tournoi* is similar to a number of thirteenth-century narratives, including *Roman de la rose* and *Violette*, but even more informative in its transmission alongside a linked collection of songs in the **Douce 308** chansonnier.[15]

---

12 The refrain melody is pitched a fourth higher in **R(mo)** than in **N(mo)**, though the remainder of the motetus lines are pitched at the same level in the two manuscripts. The pitch level of the refrain in **N(mo)** creates marginally fewer dissonances with the tenor than does the **R(mo)** pitch level.
13 Atchison, *The* Chansonnier *of Oxford Bodleian MS Douce 308*, 29–30. See also *The Old French Ballette: Oxford, Bodleian Library, MS Douce 308*, 1 *et passim*.
14 Huot, *Allegorical Play*, 138, summarizes a theory made as early as 1886 by Schwan that Douce 308 represents a collection of pieces for a *puy*.
15 In Nancy Regalado's words, the *Tournoi* and the chansonnier, in combination with two other **Douce 308** manuscript items, "constitute a complete kit of secular chivalry, linking the ideals of prowess, love, and lyric savoir faire to proper names that point to a particular local audience [in Lorraine]." Cited in *The Old French Ballette*, li. See Regalado, "Picturing the Story of Chivalry in Jacques Bretel's *Tournoi de Chauvency* (Oxford, Bodleian Library, MS Douce 308)," in *Tributes to Jonathan J. G. Alexander*, ed. S. L. Engle and G. B. Guest (London: Harvey Miller, 2006), 343, for a varied, published version of this statement that appeared after its pre-publication inclusion in *The Old French Ballette*.

The **Douce 308** motet in question, EM 389, shares its motetus refrain vdB 1463 with an anonymous *pastourelle avec des refrains, En une praele*: it appears with music in trouvère sources **KN(trv)PTX** (all copied 1270–80 in the Picardy-Artois region, with **X** probably from Arras, and **T** in Artois with a likely connection to Arras), and without music in MS **U** (known as the "Chansonnier St. Germain," whose earliest gatherings are dated to 1231 in or around Metz).[16] Because the motet source **Douce 308** does not transmit music, we cannot determine the refrain's melodic lineage. Nonetheless, given the dating of the earliest song source to 1231, and the later ones to 1270–80, the creator of EM 389 may have known the refrain (text and music) from one of them. The refrain is also found (without music) in a later narrative poem, *Court d'amours*, which depicts an aristocratic community that forms a court of law to try questions of love and to hear love complaints; it includes a sequence of thirty-three refrains, aligning it with *Renart le Nouvel*, whose final processional scene offers a sequence of thirty-five refrains.[17] *Court d'amours* appears to originate between 1277 and 1328 from Hainault, a region adjacent to Artois.[18] Its only surviving source is an early fourteenth-century manuscript, **Pa 1731**. Based on *Court d'amours*'s dating, it cannot be excluded as a possible link to EM 389, though lineage through the *pastourelle* seems more likely.

---

16 MS **T** presents several melodic variants in comparison to the nearly exact identity in **KN(trv)PX**. For discussion of MS U, see Robert Lug, "Katharer und Waldenser in Metz: Zur Herkunft der ältesten Sammlung von Trobador-Liedern (1231)," in *Okzitanistik, Altokzitanistik und Provenzalistik: Geschichte und Auftrag einer europäischen Philologie*, ed. Angelica Rieger (Frankfurt and Berlin: Lang, 2000), 249–74; and Callahan, "Collecting Trouvère Lyric at the Peripheries, 16–23.

17 Butterfield, *Music and Poetry*, 146. She also comments: "[it] bears a close resemblance to *Le Tournoi de Chauvency*. The parallels are numerous and include—apart from details of the action—the tournament, and the use of historical characters in the dancing scenes." On the *Renart le nouvel*, see Anne Ibos-Augé, "Récurrences et formules mélodiques dans le roman de *Renart le Nouvel*," Brepols Online, 257–89. https://doi.org/10.1484/M.ARTEM-EB.5.103354. Ibos-Augé says of the *Renart*, "This text also belongs to the 'inserted texts' important corpus, which appears to have been a real fad during the whole thirteenth century in northern France, beginning with Jean Renart, who wrote the *Guillaume de Dole* romance around 1228" ("Ce texte appartient par ailleurs à l'important corpus des 'romans à insertions', en vogue durant tout le XIIIe siècle en France d'oïl depuis Jean Renart, auteur du roman de *Guillaume de Dole* écrit vers 1228"), 257–58.

18 *Le Court d'Amours de Mahieu le Poirier et la suite anonyme de la "Court d'Amours,"* ed. T. Scully (Waterloo, Ont.: Wilfried Laurier University Press, 1976), xxii.

The *pastourelle*'s first verse ends with the refrain:

En une praele
m'entrai l'autrier,
Trouvai pastorele
lez son bergier.
Li bergiers la bele
vouloit besier,
Mes en fesoit ele
mult grant dangier,
Car de cuer ne l'amoit mie,
Oncor fust ce sa plevie,
Si avoit ele ami
Autre que son mari,
Car son mari, je ne sai pour quoi,
Het ele tant qu'ele s'escrioit:
*Ostez moi l'anelet du doit,
Ne sui pas marïee a droit!*[19]

whereas in the motet the refrain's lines frame the verse:

*Osteis lou moi,
L'anelet dou doi!*
Avoir pas vilains ne me doit,
Car, bien sai, cous en seroit
S'avocke moi
Longement estoit;
Departir m'an vuel orandroit,
Je ne suix par marïee a droit.[20]

If the motet did follow from the *pastourelle*, the latter's familiar encounter context, in which a man largely relates what he overhears a woman saying, has been displaced in favor of unmediated direct speech by a married woman. In the pastourelle, the narrator imparts his view of the situation at hand, whereas in the motet a woman speaks for herself, in a defiant manner, using the words *vilains* and *cous* to cast aspersions on the husband forced upon her through an arranged marriage. Within the *malmariée* motet corpus, EM 389 presents one of

---

19 The full song text appears in *Chanter m'estuet*, 52–54.
20 See Chapter 4, note 6.

the most forthright statements about how a woman could react to an arranged marriage. Hearing the refrain in this new context may have startled a listener who was familiar with it through the more distant voice of the *pastourelle* narrator.

Mo 7, 271, *Dame bele et avenant et de biau port/Fi, mari, de vostre amour!/NUS N'IERT JA JOLIS, S'IL N'AIME*, transmits three refrains, vdB 1842 and 746 (both in the *malmariée* motetus voice), and 1407 (in the French tenor). See Table 3. While vdB 1842 appears only in the Montpellier motet and its fragmentary concordance, **Vat. 1543** (probably from the end of the thirteenth century), vdB 746 is also found in a polyphonic rondeau *Fi, mari, de vostre amour* by Adam de la Halle, whose name is inextricably linked to Arras.[21] The rondeau is itself a *malmariée* text and therefore a conceit if indeed written by Adam. vdB 746 is also found in *Renart le nouvel*, whose date John Haines has reconsidered, suggesting that its first book and possibly its second (which contains refrains) might predate 1286 or even 1283.[22] Both Adam's polyphonic rondeau and the individual refrain in *Renart* appear on fols. 33rb and 167va, respectively, within **Pa 25566** (probably produced in Arras in the early 1290s), known as "Adam de la Halle" trouvère manuscript **W** and the central source of Adam's polyphonic compositions. Given that the refrain has an exactly matching identity in both appearances, the music scribe of **W** may have copied the *Renart* refrain and Adam's rondeau from a common exemplar or copied the *Renart* refrain directly from Adam's rondeau in **W**.[23] More importantly for our purposes, the refrain in the motetus of **Mo 7**, 271 carries the exact same melodic profile as its two appearances in **W**. In fact, the **Mo 7** motet shares the first few perfections of its three-voice polyphony with the opening three-voice polyphony of Adam's rondeau, though with variations.[24]

Speculating on the likely direction of transmission between Adam's rondeau *Fi, mari, de vostre amour* and the **Mo 7** motet is complicated by the motet's third refrain, vdB 1407, *Nus n'iert ja jolis, s'il n'aime*,

---

21 See Carol Symes, "The 'School of Arras' and the Career of Adam," in *Musical Culture in the World of Adam de la Halle*, ed. Jennifer Saltzstein (Leiden and Boston, MA: Brill, 2019), 21–50.
22 John Haines, *Satire in the Songs of* Renart le nouvel (Geneva: Droz, 2010), 34.
23 Jennifer Saltzstein, "Adam de la Halle's Fourteenth-Century Musical and Poetic Legacies," in Saltzstein, *Adam*, 352–63, at 355.
24 Anne Ibos-Augé, "Refrain Quotations in Adam's Rondeaux, Motets and Plays," in Saltzstein, *Adam*, 261–63; Mark Everist, "Friends and Foals: The Polyphonic Music of Adam de la Halle," Ibid., 335–38.

which appears with this music only in the tenor of **Mo** 7, 271. The refrain text also appears as the opening refrain of another polyphonic rondeau found in MS **k**, where the space left for the music has not been filled in, and in *Court d'amours II*. The dating of the surviving sources for vdB 1407 offers little guidance in establishing a transmission route: **Mo** 7 is dated to the late thirteenth century, possibly the 1290s,[25] the *Court d'amours*, a wide span of 1277–1328, and MS **k**, the early fourteenth century.

A further complication arises from the fact that vdB 1407 features in the shared polyphonic complex between Adam's *malmariée* rondeau *Fi, mari* and the **Mo** 7 motet; the motet tenor begins with the refrain *Nus n'iert ja jolis, s'il n'aime*, then follows the pattern of a *rondeau simple*, AbaAabAB.[26] Noting *Nus n'iert ja joli s'il n'aime*'s presence in the shared polyphonic complex, Everist has considered plausible two of three possible transmission scenarios: (1) the existence of a monophonic version of *Nus n'iert ja jolis, s'il s'aime* that the motet creator adopted as the motet's tenor, adding upper voices above it; Adam then reworked this complex in his rondeau *Fi, mari*; (2) the other scenario gives priority to Adam's rondeau, with the motet adopting the rondeau's opening three-voice polyphony, then composing out the tenor as a separate rondeau with the text *Nus n'iert ja jolis, s'il n'aime*; that tenor would then have circulated separately "and served as probably the middle voice of the polyphonic *rondeau* [perhaps the rondeau in MS **k**] with the same *incipit*."[27] Everist considers both scenarios problematic in that each harbors assumptions at odds with conventional practice of composing motets and rondeaux.[28] Nonetheless, he seems to lean toward the first scenario, i.e. Adam basing his rondeau on the motet, as he suggests earlier when he notes that five of the six rondeaux by Adam available for comparative investigation:

> have *refrains* that are also found in motets in *Mo* fascicle seven—a correspondence that is too substantial to be coincidental. This seems to suggest the possibility that the composers of the motets

---

25 *Grove Music Online*, "Sources, MS," offers summary dating that includes **Mo** 7: "fascs.1 and 7, plus the additions to 3 and 5, very end of 13th century (Branner: late 13th century, Everist: 1280s)." In the introduction to *The Montpellier Codex: The Final Fascicle*, ed. Bradley and Desmond, 5–6, Bradley and Desmond refer to the copying of **Mo** 7 in the 1290s.
26 Everist, "Friends and Foals," 336.
27 Ibid., 337–38.
28 Ibid.

in the seventh fascicle of *Mo* were familiar with Adam's *rondeaux*, and chose their *refrains* from that repertory, or—**perhaps more likely**—Adam was familiar with the repertory of motets from fascicle seven of *Mo*, and borrowed from them the *refrains*—and possibly in one instance a polyphonic complex—in his *rondeaux*.[29]

In her article "Choosing a Thirteenth-Century Motet Tenor," Catherine Bradley focuses on an additional piece of internal evidence that instead argues for the motet creator having borrowed from Adam's *malmariée* rondeau *Fi, mari, de vostre amour*. Looking beyond the shared opening polyphonic complex, she notes that when the motet tenor reaches its internal partial refrain *nus n'iert ja jolis*, the motetus presents over it a variant of the fifth line of Adam's rondeau: Adam's "Il me sert et nuit et jour" reads "qui me sert et nuit et jou" in the motet:

Adam's rondeau		**Malmariée motetus**	
Fi, maris, de vostre amour	vdB 746	Fi, mari, de vostre amour!	vdB 746
Car j'ai ami.		Quar j'ai aimi,	
Biaus est et de noble atour,		tel com il afiert a mi,	
Fi, maris, de vostre amour,		qui me sert et nuit et jour	
Il me sert et nuit et jour,		sanz sejour	
Pour che l'aim si,		de cuer mignot et joli.	
Fi maris de vostre amour		Vilains, vous demorés	vdB 1842
Car j'ai ami.		et je m'en vois a li!	

To quote Bradley:

> That an additional textual connection between the two compositions occurs at a structurally significant moment in "Dame Bele"/"Fi, mari"/NUS N'IERT JA JOLIS, motivated by the independent rondeau form of the tenor, arguably underlines the status of the line "qui me sert et nuit et jour" as a quotation in the motet. It is harder to explain why Adam would borrow just one additional line of a motet text for the fifth line of his rondeau.[30]

---

29 Ibid., 329. Emphasis added.
30 Catherine A. Bradley, "Choosing a Thirteenth-Century Motet Tenor: From the *Magnus liber organi* to Adam de la Halle," *JAMS* 72 (2019): 431–92, at 480; for full discussion, see pp. 475–82. Bradley acknowledges that Ludwig noted the appearance of an additional line of text from Adam's rondeau in the motet (see p. 480, n. 124). Ibos-Augé also

Bradley then offers an alternative to Everist's explanation of how the motet tenor itself came to be. Noting several differences between the tenors of the rondeau and motet in the opening perfections, she argues that the motet creator did not simply retext the beginning of Adam's rondeau tenor and then compose it out as a different rondeau. Instead, the motet creator adopted a pre-existing melody that replicated the melodic contour of Adam's tenor, namely, an anonymous rondeau *Nus n'iert ja jolis*. Bradley thus suggests double quotation within this motet—of the anonymous rondeau *Nus n'iert ja jolis* in the tenor and of Adam's refrain *Fi, mari* and its surrounding polyphonic voices. She grounds her speculation about this motet on instances of double quotation in other late thirteenth-century examples, what she calls "quotational feats."[31]

We await the discovery of a musically notated source for the rondeau *Nus n'iert ja jolis*, thereby allowing proof of Bradley's hypothesis about the genesis of the motet's tenor. In the meantime, relying on internal textual and musical features, she offers a compelling argument that the motet grew from Adam's rondeau *Fi, mari*. Viewing **Mo 7, 271**'s composite picture of three refrains, it is certain that multiple rondeaux factored into its creation and transmission in some way, with specific musical and textual features bringing it into a nexus with Adam de la Halle's rondeau as transmitted in the Arras MS **W**. For a listener familiar with Adam's *malmariée* rondeau *Fi, mari*, hearing its refrain "Fie on your love, husband! For I have a lover" (vdB 746) at the motet beginning, then an equally vehement refrain "Wretch, you will stay here, and I will go to him [her lover]!" (vdB 1842) at its end, may have been arresting because of the increased castigation of the husband. Furthermore, as discussed in Chapter 4, a listener might interpret the *malmariée* of the motet, who revels in her consummated love, as parodying both the triplum and tenor males who yearn for an unattainable woman.

The final motet whose refrain appears in both a chanson and a romance or narrative poem is **Mo 8, 325**, *S'on me regarde, s'on me regarde/Prennés i garde, s'on me regarde/HÉ MI ENFANT*, built over a French tenor incipit whose origins are unknown. **Mo 8, 325** is the only

---

noted this correspondence in "Refrain Quotations in Adam's Rondeaux, Motets and Plays," 261–62.

31 See further exploration of connections between Adam's work and **Mo 7** in Catherine A. Bradley, *Authorship and Identity in Late Thirteenth-Century Motets*, Royal Musical Association Monographs No. 39 (London and New York: Routledge, 2022), especially Chapter 1.

malmariée motet in fascicle 8 of Montpellier. The latest scholarship on this fascicle places its copying at the juncture of the thirteenth and fourteenth centuries, of likely Parisian provenance, though its production may not be typical or purely Parisian, given that its decorations cannot be matched definitively with any Parisian artist. Alison Stones raises the possibility that the fascicle's illustrations may have been the work of a northern artist operating in Paris or even that it traveled north for its decoration.[32]

The refrain transmitted in both upper voices of this motet, vdB 1531, appears with music notation in a rondeau, *Prendés i garde, s'on mi regarde*, attributed to Guillaume d'Amiens (fl. end of the thirteenth century) in trouvère manuscript **a**, which is the only manuscript to preserve his music. According to Alison Stones, the manuscript was compiled in Arras ca. 1275–80.[33] As shown in Example 1, the motet's two statements of the refrain reveal melodic variants between them, but both retain the essential pitch contour of the rondeau melody (though pitched a fifth higher).[34] The refrain also appears in *Renart le nouvel*; three of its four sources contain music, of which MS **W** presents a roughly matching melody to that of the chanson at the lower pitch level, while **Pa 372**'s melody would be considered a variant version.[35]

---

32 See Bradley and Desmond, "Introduction," *The Montpellier Codex: The Final Fascicle*, 4, which summarizes dating proposed by the volume's authors: on art historical grounds, Alison Stones proposes between 1315 and 1325, and Rebecca Baltzer favors the 1310s, probably early in that decade. Based on scribal hand, Sean Curran offers a slightly earlier date between 1290 and 1310. See Stones, "The Style and Iconography of Montpellier folio 350r," Ibid., 66–77; Baltzer, "The Decoration of Montpellier 8: Its Place in the Continuum of Parisian Manuscript Illumination," Ibid., 78–89; Curran, "A Palaeographical Analysis of the Verbal Text in Montpellier 8: Problems, Implications, Opportunities," Ibid., 32–65. Neither Stones nor Baltzer has located fascicle 8's artist in a very wide range of Parisian books.

33 Alison Stones, *Gothic Manuscripts 1260–1320* (London and Turnhout: Harvey Miller Publishers, 2013–14), Part 1, vol. 2, p. 161.

34 The variants between the motet's two statements of the refrain are attributable to their simultaneous utterance: the motetus presents the text and music phrase *prennés i garde*, while the triplum begins at the same time on the second text/music phrase *s'on me regarde*, creating an imitative effect between the two lines and requiring melodic adjustments. Also note that the chanson's repeat of the text *s'on me regarde* is changed to *trop sui gaillarde* in the motetus.

35 Mark Everist, in "Motets, French Tenors, and the Polyphonic Chanson ca. 1300," 392, n. 67, states, "With the exception of *F-Pn* fr. 1593 (which preserves an unrelated melody in unmeasured notation), all other notated sources agree closely on the melodic details of the *refrain*." As Ex. 2 shows, fr. 372's version in fact does not descend a fifth at the beginning, as the melody in MS **W** does. For a text edition based on **W**, see Jacquemart Giélée, *Renart le nouvel, publié d'après le manuscrit La Vallière (B.N.*

Example 1 Transmission of refrain vdB 1531 melody

From the refrain's combined transmission picture, we can surmise that the motet creator probably knew it from Guillaume d'Amien's rondeau or possibly from its appearance in *Renart le nouvel*.[36]

In Chapter 4 I argued for including this motet within the *malmariée* corpus because of its reference to the "jealous one," even though the marital status of the female speaker is unclear. To explore further meanings, we turn to the rondeau as the likely source of its refrain:

> *Prendés i garde,*
> *S'on me regarde!*
> *S'on mi regarde,*
> *Dites le moi.*
> *C'est tout la jus en cel boschaige:*
> *Prendéz i garde,*
> *S'on me regarde!*
> *La pastourele i gardoit vaches:*
> *Plaisans brunette a vous m'otroi!*
> *Prendés i garde,*
> *S'on me regarde!*
> *S'on mi regarde,*
> *Dites le moi.*

(Take note if anyone looks at me! If anyone looks at me, tell me. It is all down there in those woods. *Take note if anyone looks at me!* The shepherdess tends the cows: Pretty brunette, I am yours! *Take note if anyone looks at me! If anyone looks at me, tell me.*)[37]

vdB 1531 is spoken here by a male in a pastoral setting. By uttering the words *Take note if anyone looks at me! If anyone looks at me, tell me*, he signals that he is concerned about being discovered spying on the shepherdess, whom he presumably intends to prey upon. When the refrain is voiced by a woman in both upper voices of the motet (see texts in Chapter 4), it can have two meanings: she wants to know if the male she desires looks at her, but is fearful that her "daring" to unite with him will be noticed by others, a fear compounded by her concern

---

fr. 25566), ed. Henri Roussel (Paris: A & J. Picard, 1961). For the music transmitted in the three manuscripts, see Haines, *Satire in the Songs of* Renart le nouvel, 235–341.

36 In 2007, Everist gave chronological priority to the rondeau. See "Motets, French Tenors, and the Polyphonic Chanson ca. 1300," 391–98, particularly 395, n. 68.

37 The text and translation are derived, with modifications, from http://stcpress.org/pieces/prendes_i_garde, accessed on September 19, 2022.

about a "jealous one." If listeners in the late thirteenth century recognized the refrain from the rondeau, they would have been struck by how the speaker changes from a male predator to an independent-minded woman determined to exact her will in matters of love. This intergeneric play would provoke them to compare the male and female depicted in the rondeau and motet, respectively: he acts behind the scenes, while she is out in a public setting. Both want to fulfill their sexual desires, he presumably through rape, she presumably by uniting with her willing lover, though her marital status is unclear. Since both individuals could be viewed as transgressing social norms, it is difficult to determine whether parody is at play, and, if so, whether the male and/or female is its intended target.

In summary, these four *malmariée* motets that share their refrains with a song and a narrative reveal northern associations to varying degrees. EM 310 falls within a definite Artesian nexus: its two sources are copied in Artois, possibly in Arras itself, while its refrain vdB 1006 appears in a song by Perrin d'Angicourt (who had connections to Arras) within multiple sources connected to the Picardy-Artois region and one to Lorraine. EM 389 reveals a clear-cut northern association through its sole source, **Douce 308**, from Lorraine, and probably borrowed its refrain vdB 1463 from an anonymous *pastourelle avec refrains* that survives in a Lorraine source dated as early as 1231, and numerous sources from the Picardy-Artois region. Though **Mo** 7, 271 survives in no northern source, it connects through its musical and textual features to a rondeau by Adam de la Halle transmitted in the Artesian MS **W**. **Mo** 8, 325's northern connections are the least definitive: it shares its refrain vdB 1531 with a rondeau by Guillaume d'Amiens uniquely preserved in trouvère manuscript **a**, copied in or around Arras in the late thirteenth century. **Mo** 8 itself may have traveled north for its decoration, though its provenance is probably Parisian. In any case, its compiler would seem to have had access to a song collection such as MS **a**, copied in the north.

The foregoing discussion has also suggested how listeners' familiarity with the intertextual source of a refrain could affect their interpretation of a given motet to varying degrees. When the refrain of EM 310 speaks against marriage and in favor of love, a listener could hear it as allegorizing or parodying the tenor's message of divine love. The parodic reading would perhaps be reinforced should a listener recall the woman's flippant tone in the chanson and *Violette* that share its refrain. When listeners heard EM 389 in dialogue with a *pastourelle* that shares its refrain, they could perceive how the *pastourelle* narrator's detached perception of a married woman's complicated love situation shifts to a woman's unmediated diatribe against her arranged marriage and loathsome husband. **Mo** 7, 271, through its intergeneric play with Adam de la Halle's *malmariée* rondeau, could also strike a listener with its intensified castigation of the husband. For **Mo** 8, 325, a startling different meaning could surface when a listener recognized that the refrain uttered by its female speaker is voiced by a male in a rondeau: *Take note if anyone looks at me! If anyone looks at me, tell me*. In both contexts, the speakers fear repercussions because they are transgressing societal norms, but the differences are significant: whereas the male contemplates preying upon an unsuspecting shepherdess, the female is scheming to join her willing lover. A listener might hear parody in this juxtaposition.

With One or More Songs

The sixth fascicle of **Mo** is dated to the late 1270s or 1280s[38] and contains five two-voice *malmariée* motets, of which three—203, 180, and 212—are relevant to the present discussion of intertextuality with other genres.[39] In all three cases, the refrain in question survives in one or more chansons, but not in narratives. Two share the liturgical tenor *IMMOLATUS*, while the third stands apart within the *malmariée* corpus for its use of a tenor related to St. Elizabeth of Hungary.

Mo 6, 203, *Hier main jouer m'en alai/[IMMO]LATUS*, which has a concordance in **W2**, shares its refrain vdB 1856 *Vous diroiz ce que vous voudroiz, maiz j'amerai!* (You can say what you want, but I will continue to love!) with two *chansons avec des refrains* (numbered 1 and 2 in the vertical column for this refrain in Table 2). The first is the anonymous *Quant li douz tans rasouage*, transmitted in MS **U** (1231 from Lorraine) and in **Mod. R.4.4** (thirteenth century). The second *chanson avec des refrains*, *En mi mai quant s'est la saisons partie*, by the trouvère Guillaume le Vinier from Arras, is transmitted in three trouvère manuscripts: **M**, copied after 1253, probably in the 1260s or 1270s in Artois, possibly in Arras; **T**, compiled ca. 1270s in Artois, with a likely connection to Arras; and **Z**, dating from the late thirteenth or early fourteenth century, in Artois or Picardy.

Of all the sources for the two *chansons avec des refrains*, only one transmits vdB 1856 with a melody: Example 2 shows the melody found in MS **M**, at a G pitch level. The motet's two sources, **Mo** and **W2**, on the other hand, transmit a refrain melody at the C pitch level, its

---

38 See Chapter 3, note 14.
39 **Mo** 6, 233 will be discussed below in the chapter on intertextuality among motets. **Mo** 6, 243's refrain (vdB 1514) has no surviving source outside of the motet.

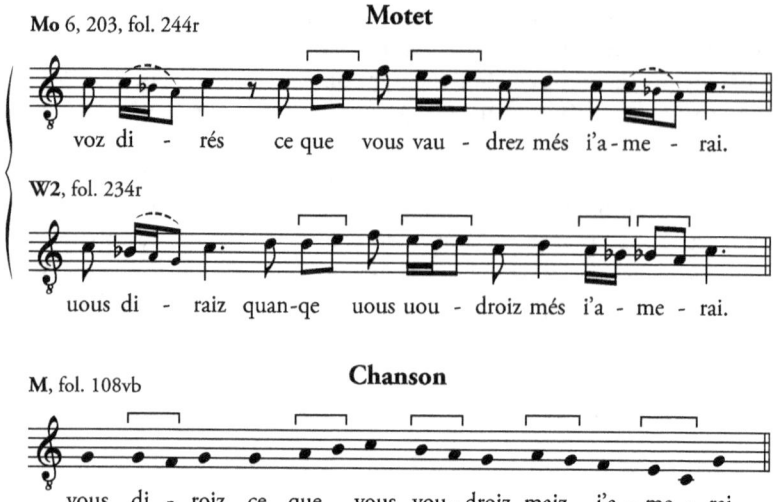

Example 2 Transmission of refrain vdB 1856 melody

identity relatively intact despite minor variants. Comparing the melody in the motet sources to that in **MS M**, one notes only a shared linear ascent and descent in the middle, a gesture perhaps too common to be considered significant. Based on the surviving evidence, one cannot speculate about the refrain melody's lineage. Nonetheless, the relative dating of the surviving chanson sources leaves open the possibility of the motet found in **Mo** and **W2** drawing upon the refrain text through one or both of the *chansons avec des refrains* that survive in sources associated with the regions of Artois, Picardy, and Lorraine.

The first *chanson avec des refrains*, *Quant li douz tans rasouage*, itself reveals aspects of *pastourelle* and *malmariée* topoi, with the added twist of an apparently moralizing outsider. The chanson begins in the manner of a *pastourelle* as a male narrator describes in the first three verses encountering a woman *simple et sage*; but her situation is unusual for a *pastourelle* in that she is being chastised by an old woman. The young woman's quoted words before she speaks to the narrator in verse 4 suggest her determination to hold on to her lover (verse 1 *amis*, verse 3 *mon ami gent*); only verse 3 mentions her husband (*ne por mon mari salvage*). vdB1856 ends the second verse:

> Droit vers la forest ramage
> M'en vois, quant j'oï lo chant,
> Plains de joie en mon corage

Et d'amorous pansement,
Si trovai tot maintenant
Une dame simple et sage
Et une vielle d'aaige,
Qui la chastoie et reprent,
Cele dit tant doucement:
"Dex, que ferai?
Vos direz quanque voldrez,   vdB 1856
Mais j'amerai."

In verse 4 the narrator approaches the young woman and a consensual sexual union seems imminent, whereupon the old woman returns and the narrator flees. When the two women converse in verse 5, the old woman seems to apologize for having interfered in the sexual tryst. This flow of ideas would suggest to a listener that a *malmariée* could and did pursue her erotic desires, including in a situation where she was confronted by a moralizing individual such as the old woman. That the young woman elicits an apology from the old woman might strike a listener as surprising and/or puzzling.[40]

The second *chanson avec des refrains* that transmits refrain vdB 1856, *En mi mai quant s'est la saisons partie*, also begins with an encounter, this time with a well-dressed woman. As was the case in *Quant li douz tans rasouage*, her husband is mentioned only once, here in verse 3:

Ja ne m'en partirai
Pour un villain que j'ai.
Ja pour mal mari, se je l'ai,   vdB 1019
Mon loial ami ne lairai.[41]

As discussed in Chapter 1, **Mo** 6, 203 itself adopts the encounter frame of a *pastourelle*, presenting a narrator who relates having overheard a conversation, in this case between a married couple. The narrator describes the lady as well-dressed, as does the narrator of *En mi mai quant s'est la saisons partie*, which might give a slight preference to this chanson as the source for the motet. In any case, the total transmission profile of vdB 1856 reveals a *pastourelle* encounter frame as a constant, intersecting with the *malmariée* topos in different ways. **Mo** 6, 203 focuses on the

---

40 My interpretation builds upon the description of the chanson offered by Johnson, "The *Malmariée* Theme in Old French Lyric," 148–50, where an edition of the text appears.
41 See P. Ménard, ed., *Les Poésies de Guillaume le Vinier* (Geneva: Droz, 1970), 140–44.

wife's defiant interaction with her husband, whereas the two *chansons avec des refrains* allow the narrator to reflect on the *malmariée* and her situation, and even engage with her in *Quant li douz tans rasouage*. In all three cases, the woman's focus is on pursuing love outside of her marriage, a sentiment captured in refrain vdB 1856. The motet takes a further step by bringing this focus into conversation with the tenor *IMMOLATUS*: the woman's unwillingness to put aside her erotic desires parodies the sentiment of Christ's self-sacrifice captured in its tenor *IMMOLATUS*.

The second motet on *IMMOLATUS*, **Mo** 6, 180, *A tort sui d'amours blasmee* /[*IMMO*]*LATUS*], contains refrain vdB 189, *A tort sui d'amours blasmee; hé Dieus, si n'ai point d'ami!* (I am wrongly criticized for loving. O God, I have no lover!), which also appears in *Quant se resjouissent oisel*, a *chanson avec des refrains* transmitted without music in four manuscripts, two of which are produced in or around Metz: **U** (ca. 1231) and **C** (1290–1300)[42]; **Mod. R.4.4** (thirteenth century); and troubadour manuscript **R(trb)** (dated no earlier than 1292).[43] The chanson's transmission as early as 1231 supports a conjecture that the motet creator may have known vdB 189 from the chanson. In turn, Bradley's supposition that the related clausula in MS **F** is a transcribed motet would imply that the motet was created as early as the 1240s and therefore that a source predating Mo once existed.

As discussed in Chapter 1, the motet text opens with vdB 189, which is spoken by a married woman to end the first verse of the chanson. Whereas the chanson concentrates on secular love, the refrain's appropriation in the motet, otherwise a *chanson pieuse*, results in a complex play on the subject of self-sacrifice: an unhappily married woman who claims not to have sought satisfaction by taking a lover parodies a woman dedicating herself to Mary, while in turn the holy woman's selflessness allegorizes Christ's sacrifice encapsulated in the tenor fragment *IMMOLATUS*.

Mo 6, 212 transmits vdB 1555, *Quant plus me bat et destraint li jalous, tant ai ge mieus en amor ma pensee* (The more the jealous one beats and oppresses me, all the more do I have love in my thoughts), which also appears in a *chanson de femme*, *Amours me fait renvoisier et chanter*, attributed to Moniot d'Arras (fl. 1213–39) in its three trouvère sources,

---

[42] Callahan, "Collecting Trouvère Lyric at the Peripheries," 16. MS **U** (BnF fr. 20050) also transmits the chansons whose refrains appear in the *malmariée* motets EM 389 and **Mo** 6, 203.

[43] Elizabeth Aubrey, *The Music of the Troubadours* (Bloomington: Indiana University Press, 1996), 46. This manuscript alone attributes the chanson to Thibaut de Blaison of Poitou.

MTa, all connected to Artois.[44] Moniot's early thirteenth-century career, coupled with the dating of these sources reasonably close to the copying of **Mo**'s sixth fascicle, allows that the creator of the motet may have known the refrain from the chanson. In the only chanson source with melody, MS **M**, the melody's identity is intact.[45] Another pertinent factor in **Mo** 6, 212's transmission is that its creator knew the motet *Un chant renvoisie* on the same tenor, as noted in Chapter 3. Significantly, *Un chant revoisie* appears uniquely in **ArsB**, dated to the 1270s and long thought to have been copied in northern France, and in Picardy in particular. But Alison Stones has recently proposed a center of manuscript production in the Artois region, perhaps from Thérouanne, St-Omer, or Arras.[46] These various threads indicate that the creator of **Mo** 6, 212 could have had access to both the chanson refrain and the motet that shares its tenor through sources associated with Artois.

As discussed in Chapter 3, Bradley's interpretation of **Mo** 6, 212 calls upon its use of a chanson refrain, vdB 1555, about beatings by a jealous one to suggest an analogy with St. Elizabeth of Hungary, to whom the tenor is dedicated. For a listener who recognized the liturgical tenor, connecting it to the motetus message about the physical beatings experienced by a married woman may have proven difficult, and knowing the refrain's chanson context would probably not have helped. A listener had to be aware of St. Elizabeth's reputed beatings by her spiritual guardian to make an allegorical connection to the beatings undergone by the *malmariée*: St. Elizabeth's beatings led her closer to God, while the female speakers in Moniot d'Arras's chanson and in the motet suggest that their beatings by their husbands drove

---

44 As noted above, Stones believes that MS **a** was compiled specifically in Arras ca. 1275–80.

45 vdB 1555 also appears in a treatise entitled *Quinque incitamenta ad Deum amandum ardenter* by Gerard of Liège (ca. 1250), which quotes secular refrains within a sacred context where God appears as a lover made jealous by readers who devote themselves to the "God of Love." See Barbara Newman, *God and the Goddesses: Vision, Poetry, and Belief in the Middle Ages* (Philadelphia: University of Pennsylvania Press, 2005), 153.

46 Alison Stones, Appendix IV, "Illustrated Miracles de Nostre Dame Manuscripts Listed by Stylistic Attribution and Attributable Manuscripts whose MND Section is Unillustrated," in *Gautier de Coinci: Miracles, Music, and Manuscripts*, ed. Kathy M. Krause and Alison Stones, Medieval Texts and Cultures of Northern Europe 13 (Turnhout: Brepols, 2006), 374, cited in Bradley, *Polyphony in Medieval Paris*, 189–90. As Bradley notes, the tenor *DECANTATUR* is derived from an Office cultivated in Cambrai, preserved with music in the Cambrai antiphoner of the 1290s and in text-only manuscripts of northern French and Flemish provenance. If **ArsB** was produced in Arras, the proximity to Cambrai is significant for the motet's creation.

them closer to their lovers. **Mo** 6, 212 thus uses the *malmariée* refrain to go beyond the issue of marriage and offer a broader insight about human nature: physical abuse may or may not have its intended effect.

In summary, three *malmariée* motets in fascicle 6 of **Mo** built on Latin tenors transmit a refrain that appears in a chanson(s). **Mo** 6, 203 is part of a refrain nexus with two *chansons avec des refrains*; all three incorporate elements of the *pastourelle* and *malmariée*. In the *chansons*, the narrator largely gives us his view of the *malmariée*'s situation, even engaging with the *malmariée* in one of them, whereas in the motet he overhears the woman's defiant answer in a heated exchange with her husband. A listener who knew one or both of the *chansons* could recognize the shift in perspective. But the woman's message is the same in all three pieces: she intends to pursue love outside of her marriage. **Mo** 6, 180 complicates its borrowing of a chanson refrain, whose married female speaker denies having a lover, by continuing as a *chanson pieuse*. Thus the motet invites a "knowing" listener to make additional comparisons between the married woman, the woman in the *chanson pieuse* who dedicates herself selflessly to Mary, and the self-sacrificing Christ of the tenor. **Mo** 6, 212 stands apart within the *malmariée* corpus because of its tenor on St. Elizabeth of Hungary and its emphasis on the effect of beatings in various contexts, including that of the *malmariée*.

With respect to transmission issues, **Mo** 6, 212 has the most suggestive connections to a northern region because it shares its uncommon tenor and some other features with another motet found in **ArsB**, a source dated to the 1270s and probably produced in the Artois region. For **Mo** 6, 203 and 180, their northern connections are limited to their sharing refrains with a song composed by a northern composer and/or transmitted in northern sources.

With a Narrative Poem

The final work which shares its refrain with another genre but not a motet is the Assumption motet, **Mo** 5, 169, *Li jalous par tout son fustat/ Tuit cil qui sunt enamourat /VERITATEM*. Its refrain vdB 1822, *Tuit cil qui sunt enamourat, viegnent dançar, li autre non* (All of those who are in love may come and dance, but not the others), sounds twice in its motetus, which unfolds as a rondeau. The second time *dancer* is replaced by *avant* (come foreward). As noted in Chapter 2, this refrain also appears in *La Court de Paradis*, a narrative poem written at the end of the thirteenth century, which contains refrain insertions within the context of a *carole* performed before the Queen of Heaven.

According to Ibos-Augé, these insertions function as entertainment in the course of danced episodes.[47] *La Court de Paradis* is transmitted in three sources: **Pa 837** (northern France, end of thirteenth century, after 1276), **Pa 25532** (end of thirteenth century), and **Pa 1802**. Only **Pa 25532** contains music, and was perhaps produced at the abbey of St-Médard de Soissons, approximately sixty miles northeast of Paris. The melody's identity is intact in the motet and **Pa 22532**. Given the dating of **Mo** fascicle 5 to the late 1270s or 1280s and the imprecise dating of **Pa 25532** and **Pa 837** to the end of the thirteenth century, a definite chronology does not emerge from the surviving sources.

The double Latin motet concordance **Mo** 4, 64, *Post partum virgo mansisti* (469)/*Ave, regina glorie* (470)/*VERITATEM*, sheds additional light on the transmission picture. The duplum text *Ave regina glorie* makes a clear reference to Mary's assumption into Heaven (*qui [Dominum] te assumpsit hodie ad ethereum thalamum*), bringing this version directly into dialogue with the feast day to which *VERITATEM* belongs, whereas the French texts of **Mo** 5, 169 relate in a more roundabout way to the liturgical source, as discussed in Chapter 2. Although this fact might suggest that the double Latin version was written first, the rondeau structure of the motetus (text and music) argues for giving chronological priority to the French version in **Mo** 5, 169.[48] The direction of borrowing between **Mo** 5, 169 and the *Paradis* remains unclear.[49]

Mark Everist concluded that this motet cannot be classed as a member of a genre he calls the "Artesian rondeau motet" because of its idiosyncratic features that set it apart from a distinct group of eight

---

47 Anne Ibos-Augé provides an in-depth discussion of the work and its sources in "Les Refrains de la 'Court de Paradis': Variance et coherence des insertions lyriques dans un poème narrative du XIIIe siècle," *Revue de Musicologie* 93 (2007), 229–67, especially 233.

48 In "The Dialectic between Occitania and France in the Thirteenth Century," *Early Music History* 16 (1997): 1–53, at 8–16, Elizabeth Aubrey summarizes István Frank's work on this motet, particularly his arguments for dating the French version first. She expands somewhat upon his arguments without concluding that the matter is settled. Frank's article is "Tuit cil qui sunt enamourat" (Notes de philologie pour l'étude des origines lyriques, II), *Romania* 297 (1954): 98–108.

49 The refrain appears twice in the motetus of **Mo** 5, 169: the first time its ending on *autre non* matches that of **Mo** 4, 64 (G C C), and the second time it matches that in the *Pardis* source, **Pa 25532** (G A B C). Because the *Paradis* ending involves a common stepwise filling-in, its appearance as the final gesture in **Mo** 5, 169 may not be significant. Frank (cited in previous note) believed that the *Paradis* version came first.

motets transmitted in trouvère MSS **M** and **T**.[50] Elizabeth Aubry has countered one of these features, its apparent "parody of Provençal music and verse structures"; she argued,

> The presence of occitanisms in the texts of the double motet seems to point to a desire to evoke southern sounds, but direct imitation of specific pieces or of a formal structure [associated with Occitanian provenance] is not clearly established.[51]

In any case, given Everist's acknowledgment that the motet shares some stylistic traits with the Artesian rondeau motet, and the fact that its refrain (text and music) survives in a *Paradis* manuscript from northeast of Paris, we conjecture that the creator of **Mo 5, 169** may well have had access to sources compiled in northern France.

Concluding Remarks

By way of summary, eight *malmariée* motets share their refrains with other genres, but not with other motets. All eight use refrains with some degree of connection to the Artois region or other northern French locales. Nonetheless, the transmission of the eight motets themselves matches the profile of this entire corpus: clearly implicated are the Parisian-produced **Mo** and **W2**, and several manuscripts compiled in northern France: the Artesian **R(mo)** and **N(mo)**, and **Douce 308** from Lorraine. For the six motets in this group transmitted in **Mo**, a Parisian lineage beyond **Mo** is evident in **Mo 6, 203**, which has a concordance with **W2**, and in **Mo 6, 180** which relates to a clausula in **F**, though the present scholarly view is that the clausula postdates the motet. **Mo 5, 169**'s concordance with a Latin double motet in another of its fascicles (**Mo 4, 64**) reveals the creative interchange within motets of this Parisian source. Of the three remaining motets, **Mo 6, 212** suggests a possible northern connection that is not dependent on its shared refrain with another genre: its creator knew another motet on the same unusual tenor *DECANTATUR* (for a feast observed in Cambrai) that is preserved in **ArsB**, a source that probably emanated from the Artois region.

With respect to their content, these eight motets reveal that a motet creator changed the meaning of a given refrain to varying degrees as it moved between a song or narrative and a motet. The simplest kind

---

50 Mark Everist, "The Rondeau Motet: Paris and Artois in the Thirteenth Century," *Music and Letters* 69 (1988): 1–22, at 18–19.
51 Aubry, "Dialectic between Occitania and France," 16.

of appropriation occurs in EM 310. Its refrain features a woman privileging love over marriage, which, on its own, could have triggered an allegorical or parodic reading of the tenor about divine love conveyed through the Holy Spirit. But a listener's recall of the flippant tone of the refrain in chanson/narrative sources may have tipped the scales toward a parodic interpretation.

Three of this subgroup of *malmariée* motets involve intergeneric play with the *pastourelle*. EM 389 (transmitted as a single French text) probably derives its refrain from a *pastourelle* in which the narrator relates overhearing a woman protesting her arranged marriage. In the motet context, her words have a greater emotional effect because she speaks directly, without mediation, and adds negative descriptors for the husband, giving a listener a sense of her vehement reaction. **Mo** 6, 203 fits into a nexus with two *chansons avec des refrains*; all three combine an encounter frame familiar from the *pastourelle* with the *malmariée* topos. Although the motet reveals a perceptible shift from the narrator's viewpoint to the woman's voice, the refrain message is the same in all three pieces: she intends to pursue love outside of her marriage. Within the motet context, the woman's words take on another level of meaning as they suggest a parody of the *IMMOLATUS* tenor message of self-sacrifice. In **Mo** 8, 325 (on a French tenor), a dramatic change in a refrain's meaning occurs when a male speaks it in a pastoral setting versus a woman in a public setting: "Take note if anyone looks at me! If anyone looks at me, tell me." He fears being caught preying upon a shepherdess as he presumably contemplates rape, whereas the woman fears being seen as she meets up with a willing lover. Though both are transgressing social norms, his contemplated act of violence in the rondeau imparts to the refrain a disturbing undertone that is not apparent in the motet. Whether parody was intended remains unclear.

The four remaining motets that share their refrains with a chanson or narrative treat the refrain's message in individualistic ways. **Mo** 7, 271 (with a French tenor) definitely relates to a rondeau by Adam de la Halle, with the rondeau's message intensified in the motet setting: their shared opening refrain, which expresses the wife's defiance as she tells her husband directly about her lover, is complemented in the motet by a closing refrain in which she castigates her husband in very strong terms, heightening her sense of defiance. But, in addition to this change within the *malmariée* voice itself, that voice also parodies the concept of aristocratic love presented in the other two motet voices, creating a rich interplay of textual meanings.

Mo 6, 180, another motet on *IMMOLATUS*, uses a *malmariée* refrain from a *chanson avec des refrains* to begin a text that is primarily a *chanson pieuse*. The intergeneric play of a secular chanson refrain in which a married woman denies having a lover and a chanson that focuses on a woman's dedication to Mary creates both levels of parody and allegory in relationship to the tenor message of Christ's self-sacrifice.

Mo 6, 212, built upon a tenor chant for the feast day of St. Elizabeth of Hungary, uses a *malmariée* refrain from a chanson to trigger in a listener familiar with St. Elizabeth's life story a connection between the beating of a *malmariée* by her husband and of St. Elizabeth by her spiritual advisor. This allegorical reading leads to a broader reflection on the differing effects of physical abuse: pushing a woman away from the husband and toward a lover in the case of marriage, but drawing her closer to God in the case of a profession of faith.

Finally, **Mo** 5, 169 (on the tenor *VERITATEM*) relates to the *malmariée* topos in a relatively indirect manner. Lacking a female voice, its third-person point-of-view mentions jealous ones who are excluded from a secular love celebration. Mention of a celebration and jealous ones may evoke thoughts of a May fest, a site where wives were thought to give expression to their discontent and desire for love, to the exclusion of jealous husbands. The refrain shared by **Mo** 5, 169 and the narrative *Court de Paradis*, which speaks of separating out those who love from those who cannot, becomes particularly rich with implications within the motet context: the idea of married women excluding their husbands parodies the mystical love celebration captured in the Assumption tenor as Christ joyously united with Mary as His Bride upon her arrival in Heaven. A more specific level of parody arises when the dissatisfied, jealous husband contrasts with the devoted Bridegroom of the tenor.

6 Motet Refrains Shared with Other Motets

As shown in Table 1, column 6, a number of the *malmariée* motets share their refrains with other motets, although not necessarily to the exclusion of intertextuality with other genres. Within Tables 4–7 (Appendix A), the motets are indicated by motet 1, motet 2, etc., in the vertical column below the relevant refrain number. The following discussion examines the intertextual context of three motets on the tenor *PORTARE:* (1) **Mo 6**, 233; (2) **Mo 5**, 148; and (3) **Mo 5**, 142, which shares refrains with another *malmariée* motet, **Mo 2**, 23 on *ET GAUDEBIT.* The chapter ends with a discussion of the intertextual context of **Mo 2**, 30 on *FIAT.*

Mo 6, 233 *Hyer main chevauchoie/PORTARE*

Mo 6, 233's motetus relates a man overhearing an unhappily married woman state, "If I dared, I would take a lover" (vdB 1691). As discussed in Chapter 2, the refrain suggests a parodic interpretation in relationship to the tenor *PORTARE*: the woman's less than wholehearted engagement in her marriage contrasts with the intense devotion of Mary to Christ epitomized in the tenor.

Evidence related to the intertextual appearance of its refrain supports this interpretation. As Table 4 (Appendix A) indicates, the *PORTARE* motet **Mo 6, 233** (motet 1) has a concordance in **N(mo)** (fol. 194v), compiled ca. 1270s in Artois, with a likely connection to Arras.[1] **N(mo)**'s next folio, 195r–v, transmits a second motet (motet 2)

---

1 *Grove Music Online*, "Sources, MS," dates the compilation of MS **N(mo)** to the 1270s or 1280s. Judith Peraino likewise writes of its compilation in the 1270s or 1280s in her essay "Taking *Notae* on King and Cleric: Thibaut, Adam, and the Medieval Readers of the *Chansonnier de Noailles* (T-*trouv.*)," in Saltzstein, *Adam*, 121. In his "Introduction" to *Motets from the Chansonnier de Noailles*, ed. Gaël

that also contains vdB 1691, *Cele m'a s'amour* (433), built on another Assumption tenor (M34): *Alleluia. Hodie Maria virgo celos ascendit. Gaudete, quia cum Christo regnat.* (Alleluia. Today the Virgin Mary ascended into Heaven. Rejoice, for she reigns with Christ.)[2] In his study of **N(mo)**, Gaël Saint-Cricq comments on the importance of the Assumption feast in the rituals undertaken by the Carité, Arras's confraternity of jongleurs and townspeople, and observes that the confraternity's devotion to the Virgin coincides with a high proportion of motets in **N(mo)** with Assumption tenors.[3] Huot identifies a cluster of motets within **N(mo)** linked specifically to the Assumption *Alleluia Hodie Maria*: three short motets whose tenors are based on successive portions of the chant, numbered according to Saint-Cricq's edition: *Alleluia*, no. 60; *Hodie*, no. 62; and *Gaudete*, no. 67, while *Cele m'a s'amour*, no. 84, uses nearly the entire chant. Huot speculates that this cluster of motets forms a male/female amatory dialogue parodying the Assumption liturgy, which, as already shown in the *Alleluia. Veni electa mea*, draws on the Song of Songs, itself a dialogue between *sponsa* and *sponsus*.[4]

Fleshing out Huot's speculation, one notes that the speakers for the three short motets, nos. 60, 62, and 67, are respectively male, female, and female (see texts and translations in Appendix B). All declare their devotion to a lover: the male of no. 60 reflects on the pains of love (*maus d'amer*) in the rhetoric of the *grand chant courtois*, suggesting an unrequited or at least unfulfilled love; the female speakers of nos. 62 and 67 on the other hand reveal a sense of joy and satisfaction in their love pursuits: "Gaily I go there, to my lover; thus should one go to her lover" and "I have found a sweetheart to my liking, worthy and wise and refined. He considers me his sweetheart, so my life will be prolonged." For a majority of no. 84, *Cele m'a s'amour*, a *cento* motet that includes twelve refrains, a male vows to persist in his love for a particular woman despite the pain caused by his unfulfilled love.[5] But its concluding lines are spoken by a woman who reveals her own

---

Saint-Cricq, with Eglal Doss-Quinby and Samuel N. Rosenberg (Middleton, WI, 2017), xviii, Saint-Cricq speculates that "collections 1–3, including the motets, were copied between the late 1260s and the late 1270s". Accounting for the divergent opinions, I have adopted c. 1270s for its compilation.

2 This motet is discussed in Mark Everist, *French Motets in the Thirteenth Century: Music, Poetry and Genre* (Cambridge: Cambridge University Press, 1994), 121–25.

3 Saint-Cricq, "Introduction," xxxii–xxxv.

4 Huot, Allegorical Play, 82–90.

5 Only the opening refrain, vdB 314, suggests the woman is receptive: *She has granted me her love, the one who's won my heart and body.*

love-induced pain, and her temptation to take a lover, using these two refrains:

Je les senc,	*I feel them,*	vdB 1059
les tres dous maus d'amer!	*the very sweet pains of love!*	
Se j'osoie,	*If I dared,*	vdB 1691
je feroie ami.	*I'd take a lover.*[6]	

For the sake of argument, we can imagine that no. 84 falls last within the motet cluster, and thus its refrain vdB 1691 would be the final sounding text. Such a positioning invites a less than clear-cut reading of the entire cluster. For nos. 62 and 67, one can interpret the female's unequivocal joy in her union with her lover allegorically in relation to the Song of Songs and Mary's love for Christ, both conveyed within the Assumption liturgy, whereas the woman speaking at the end of no. 84 suggests a transgressive act. As she is tempted to fulfill her own desires, her utterances amount to a parody of Mary's selfless love for Christ. In retrospect, one then asks whether the female speakers of the short motets, seemingly self-satisfied, might offer a twofold parody: of Mary's selfless role, and of the male speakers in nos. 60 and 84, whose desire for love remains unfulfilled.

But even in a scenario where *Cele m'a s'amour* was not performed last, its ending refrain vdB 1691 still invites a parodic reading, because its message of a woman wishing to take a lover, which could include a married woman looking outside her marriage, clashes with that of the underlying Assumption chant: *Alleluia. Hodie Maria* paints an image of Christ co-reigning harmoniously with his Bride Mary for all eternity. Thus, returning to our starting point, the appearance of this refrain within *Hyer main chevauchoie/PORTARE*, spoken by a married woman, is suggestive, given that it falls one folio apart from *Cele m'a s'amour* in MS N(mo). Both motets use Assumption chants in their tenors and end their texts with refrain vdB 1691. In both, the woman's final words seem to parody the Assumption liturgy in which Mary, the Mother of Christ, has become His steadfast Bride after her assumption into Heaven. The married woman of *Hyer main chevauchoie/ PORTARE* counters that image in a particularly powerful manner as she complains about how her husband dominates her. Furthermore, this motet surprises its listener through its intergeneric play: hearing

---

6 See Appendix B for full text and translation of no. 84.

its opening encounter gambit familiar from the *pastourelle*, a listener would expect the narrator to come upon a shepherdess, but instead he finds a *malmariée* who contemplates taking a lover.

The direction of borrowing between the two motets is difficult to establish. **Mo** 6, 233 (motet 1) has a concordance in **N(mo)**, while *Cele m'a s'amour* (motet 2) is found on **N(mo)** and in **W2**. As shown in Example 3, the refrain appears with essentially the same melodic profile and text underlay in both sources of motet 1 and in motet 2 as transmitted in **W2**. **N(mo)**'s transmission of the refrain differs: on s*e j'osie*, **N(mo)** pitches the first neighbor-note figure a third higher, but then picks up the B A G F descent found in the other sources and continues with a matching contour, though the placement of syllables across the melody is shifted. Based on this musical evidence, one cannot reach a firm conclusion on whether the creator of *Hyer main chevauchoie/ PORTARE* may have known the refrain from its appearance in the two-voice *cento* motet or vice versa.

Saint-Cricq has provided the most recent scholarship on this manuscript nexus of **N(mo)**, **W2**, and **Mo**. He argues that **N(mo)** is not only a compilation of motets created in Artois, but also "presents a solid

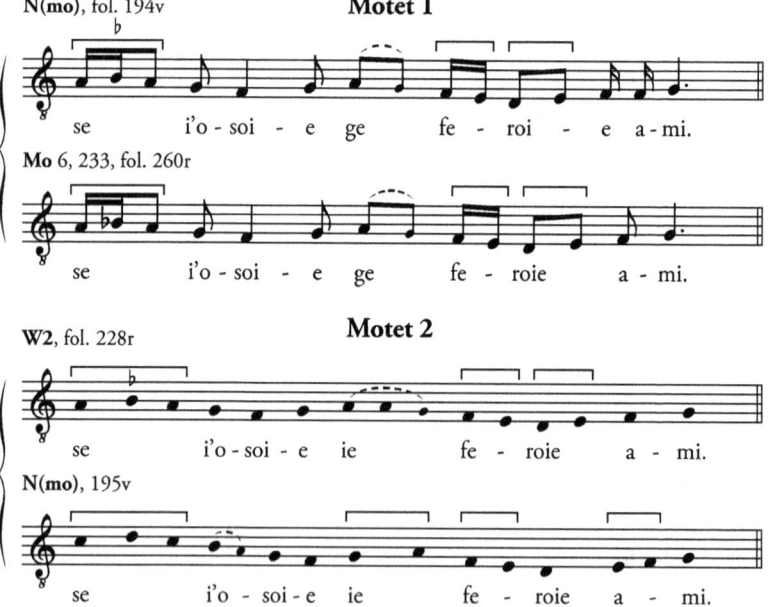

Example 3 Transmission of refrain vdB 1691 melody

body of motets originating in Parisian manuscripts."[7] He further notes that the liturgical provenance of the melismas in **N(mo)** is "by and large comparable to that of the Parisian collections in fascicle 6 of **Mo** and fascicle 10 of **W2**, showing the same major presence of tenors from Easter and Assumption liturgies." He thus suggests that **N(mo)** drew upon Parisian collections. He notes a flow "in the opposite direction," from Artois to Paris, in a handful of Artesian works that are included in Parisian codices, especially in **W2**. He does not speculate how **Mo** fits into the picture, though because **Mo** postdates **W2**, we know that **W2** could not have borrowed from **Mo**.[8]

A broader look at transmission patterns of the *malmariée* motets and their refrains sheds a bit more light on this manuscript nexus (see Table 1, columns 5 and 6). **Mo** 6, 233's sole concordance is **N(mo)**, fol. 194v, while the *cento* motet that shares its refrain vdB 1691 appears on **N(mo)**'s next folio (fol. 195r–v) and in **W2** on fols. 227v–228r. Another *PORTARE* motet, **Mo** 5, 148, shares its refrain vdB 750 with **Mo** 5, 97 (in 3 voices), which has a two-voice concordance in **N(mo)** and in **W2** on the same or adjacent folios to those of the *cento* motet just discussed (fol. 194v and fol. 228v, respectively). Thus, two *malmariée* motets based on *PORTARE* (**Mo** 6, 233 and 5, 148), transmitted in fascicles of **Mo** believed to be copied in the late 1270s or 1280s, share refrains with additional motets that appear in **N(mo)** and **W2** at most a folio apart in each manuscript. With this tantalizing piece of evidence in hand, we now complicate the picture by examining the transmission of all the refrains in **Mo** 5, 148.

Mo 5, 148 *Si com[e] aloie jouer/Deduisant com fins amourous/PORTARE*

This three-voice *malmariée* motet on the tenor *PORTARE* possesses a highly organized structure that incorporates four refrains: vdB 532, 750, 1489, and 1781 (see Table 5 (Appendix A) and Example 4). Notably, the tenor fragment is notated a fifth lower than usual, starting on F and ending on C, versus a customary beginning on C and ending on G. This feature factors into **Mo** 5, 148's relationship to other sources that share its refrains, as will be discussed below.

---

7 Saint-Cricq, "Introduction," xxi. He thus steps beyond the caution urged by Mark Everist in relating **N** to **Mo** in *French Motets in the Thirteenth Century*, 125. Everist refers to the "substantial geographical divide which separates Montpellier (Paris) from Noailles and Roi (Artois/Arras)."
8 Saint-Cricq, "Introduction," xxxii.

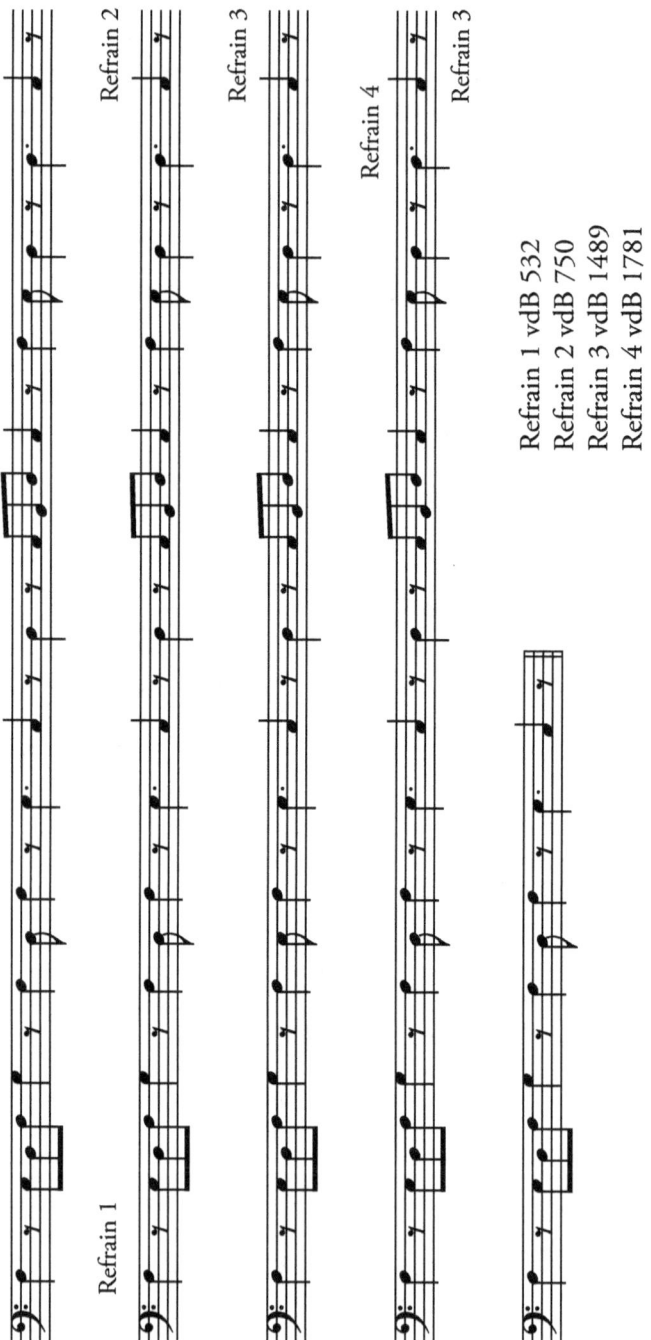

Example 4 Scheme of refrain entrances for **Mo** 5, 148

Within the triplum, three ladies (*dames*) speak: the first two respectively utter refrains 1 and 2, and the third, refrains 3 and 4 (full French texts and translations appear in Chapter 2):

> As I went out to amuse myself the other day, I found three ladies.
> One was moved by a gay heart to sing:
> (**1-vdB 532**) *"God, I dare not go to my sweetheart! How shall I have mercy?"*
> Then with nary a pause:
> (**2-vdB 750**) *"I have found true love and I will keep watch over it."*
> And then with a joyous heart:
> (**3-vdB 1489**) *"May it please God that each of us have the skin of her jealous husband;*
> would that my sweetheart were with me!
> (**4-vdB 1781**) *My whole heart laughs with joy when I see him.* I offer myself entirely to him."

Refrain 1 Dex, je n'i os aler; avrai je ja merci? (**vdB 532**)

The text of this refrain, "God, I dare not go! Shall I obtain mercy?," is transmitted in a *chanson avec des refrains, Quant je voi esté,* by Perrot de Douai, in trouvère sources **KN(trv)X** (dated 1270–80, linked to the Picardy-Artois region), none of which provides music for the refrain.[9] The refrain also appears in two other motets (on different tenors) within fascicle 5: **Mo** 5, 80 (motet 2) and **Mo** 5, 101 (motet 3). They possess a shared core of text and music (see Example 5). Significantly, in all three motets, the second line of the refrain now begins with *com[m]ent,* "*How* shall I obtain mercy?," revealing an intertextual motet nexus, even allowing that one or more of the motet creators may have known the melody from the chanson tradition.

In **Mo** 5, 80, *Je m'en vois, ma douce amie* (11)/*Tieus a mout le cuer hardi* (12)/OMNES (M1), a man speaks in the *grand chant courtois* tradition about the woman of his affections, who has not shown an interest in him (see bold text):

> Tieus a mout le cuer hardi
> en quidier et en penser,
> qui l'a couart et failli,
> quant ce vient au demoustrer.
> Ce voit on bien esprover
> en amor, por moi le di,

---

9 Nothing is known about Perrot de Douai.

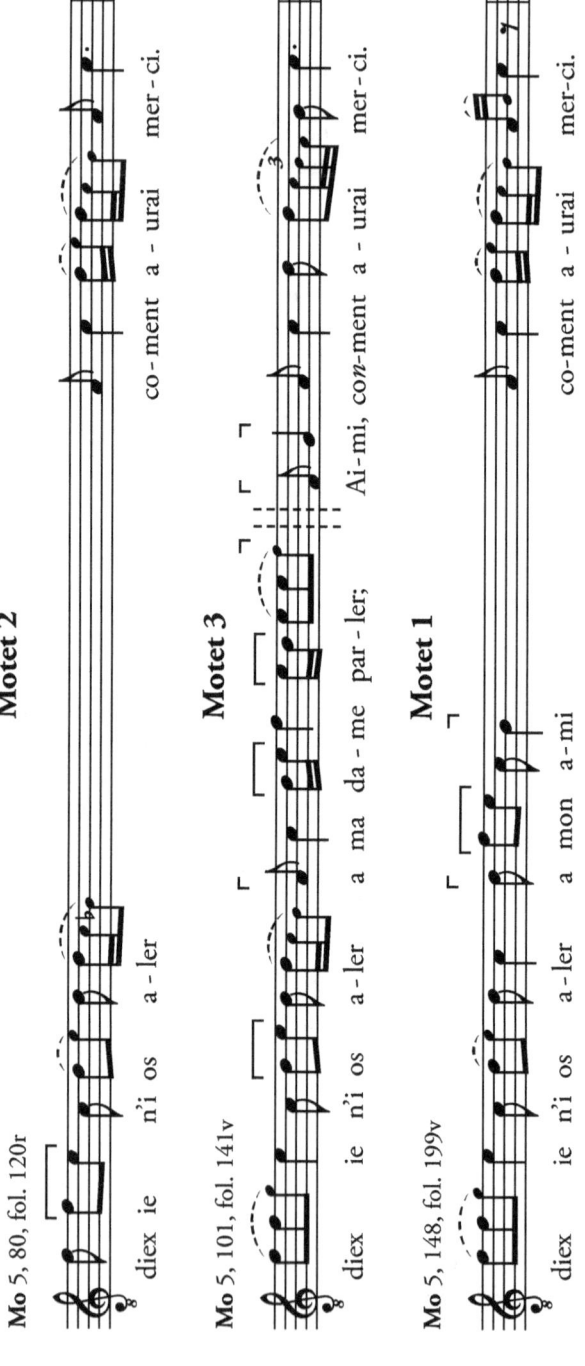

Example 5 Transmission of refrain vdB 532 melody

qui sospris sui d'amer
cele, qui onques ne vi
ses **ieuz envers moi torner.**
Si ne la puis oblier,
par Diu, ce poise mi,
car je l'aim tant et criem si,
que ne sai, comment a li
voise parler.
Dieus, je n'i os aler!
Coment avrai merci?

(One who has a brave heart when it's a question of thought and intention is faint-hearted and cowardly when it comes to action. This can be clearly proven in love, and I speak for myself, who am captured by the love of **one whose eyes have never rested upon me**. I cannot forget her, by God, and this grieves me, for I love her and fear her so that I know not how I can go speak to her. *God, I dare not go! How shall I obtain mercy?*)

The refrain repeats the preceding line's sentiment of the lover fearing to reveal himself to the apparently indifferent lady, then presents his query about how to obtain her mercy.

In **Mo** 5, 101, *Dieus, je n'i os aler a ma dame parler* (554)/*Amours, qui m'uprist de ses gcus* (555)/*ET SUPER* (M66), on the other hand, the two halves of the refrain provide a frame for the triplum, again spoken by a male whose love aspirations are thwarted:

Dieus, je n'i os aler
a ma dame parler;
tant redout la gent haïe,
qui d'envie
fondant va por la joie,
dont amant sont soustenu.
Je vaudroie,
que mesdisant
fuissent sourt et avugle et mu!
Ma dame les crient tant,
que de moi s'en va eslongnant.
Aimi, comment avrai merci?

(*God, I dare not go speak to my lady*; that is how much I fear those cursed ones who out of envy destroy the joy which sustains lovers. I would like all slanderers to be deaf, blind, and dumb! My lady fears them so much that she is distancing herself from me. *Alas, how shall I obtain mercy?*)

The refrain's core words *Dieus, je n'i os aler* (God, I dare not go) are followed by the appendage *a ma dame parler* (speak to my lady) (see open brackets above staff in Example 5). The next lines (not shown in Example 5, but indicated by the vertical dotted lines after *parler*) inform us that the threat of envious slanderers gives rise to both the lover's hesitation and the lady's distancing herself from him, that is, she too fears the spies. Despite the introduction of a third party into this lover's lament, the mercy he seeks in his concluding "how shall I obtain mercy?" is presumably still the lady's. One additional word, *aimi* (alas), is added before *comment*, the word common to the three motets.

In the *malmariée* context of **Mo** 5, 148, the wife who utters this refrain also adds different words after "I dare not go": in contrast to the male speaker of **Mo** 5, 101 who specifies "speak to my lady," the wife in **Mo** 5, 148 adds "to my lover" (*a mon ami!*), set to a different short musical interpolation (see open brackets above staff in Example 5), followed immediately by the rhetorical question "How shall I obtain mercy?"

Noting the presence of an interjected textual/musical phrase in two of the motets within this complex, Jennifer Saltzstein raised the question of whether "the interjections were inserted into the shorter version of the refrain or the interjected refrain could be the original, making the other refrain a pared-down version." She concluded: "The linguistic status of an interjection makes the former explanation the more logical one, however."[10] Based on this assumption, **Mo** 5, 80 (with no interpolation) would be the likely starting point among the three motets. Might the issue of a gendered "voice" and musical evidence support or refute this assumption and help clarify a relative chronology among the three motets?

Given the predominant male voice in the chanson repertory and within the *grand chant courtois* rhetoric of French motet upper voices generally, one is tempted to prioritize chronologically the male voice speaking in **Mo** 5, 80 and 101 as opposed to the female voice in **Mo** 5, 148. But it seems premature to make such an assumption until additional research is carried out on the presence of the female voice within motet and chanson intertextual clusters.

Turning to musical evidence (see Example 5), two factors suggest that **Mo** 5, 148 may well be the last motet in this complex. First, though each motet is based on a different tenor snippet, the refrain appears at the same pitch level in all three. Significantly, while **Mo** 5, 80 and 101 notate their respective tenors (*OMNES* and *ET SUPER*) at their usual pitch locations, **Mo** 5, 148 transposes the *PORTARE* chant incipit. Taking only refrain vdB 532 into consideration at this point, we

---

10 Saltzstein, *The Refrain and the Rise of the Vernacular*, 27, note 66.

can speculate that the tenor transposition allows **Mo** 5, 148 to accommodate the refrain at its commonly notated pitch level.[11] Second, a comparison of the melodic profile of the refrain in the three motets is most suggestive of their possible chronology and interaction: **Mo** 5, 148 shares variants with both **Mo** 5, 80 and 101. **Mo** 5, 148 begins with the same two perfections as **Mo** 5, 101, ornamental in character, whereas its setting of *coment avrai merci* agrees exactly with that of **Mo** 5, 80. The interpolated fragment in **Mo** 5, 148 arguably shares its initial contour with **Mo** 5, 101 (C D F E). This combined evidence suggests that the creator of **Mo** 5, 148 may have known both **Mo** 5, 80 and 101.

Allowing for continued questions about the exact chronology among **Mo** 5, 80, 101, and 148, one nonetheless notes the skillful rhetorical use of refrain vdB 532 at the same pitch level in three different motets within the same fascicle (5) of **Mo**, all with the added word *comment*. This usage illuminates an aesthetic grounded in the creative reuse of materials within the motet genre. By changing the gender of the speaker, the motets offer nuanced views of the experience of love: the male in the motetus of **Mo** 5, 80 doesn't act, ostensibly because he fears the woman's indifference and possible rejection[12]; the male in the triplum of **Mo** 5, 101 doesn't act because he fears slanderers, and claims that the same fear causes the woman to distance herself from him. Given that this view is spoken by a man, we wonder whether the lady's indifference is in fact a ruse to fool outsiders, or might the man delude himself in thinking it is so. In **Mo** 5, 148's triplum, where three different women speak, the first says she fears approaching her lover, without saying why. These different scenarios, heard within an intertextual nexus, lead us to reflect on an array of possible obstacles in matters of love: a woman's indifference to the suitor, her fear of being caught, or possibly her moral sense; a man's fear of rejection or exposure; and external obstacles such as a jealous husband, slanderer, or other societal constraints.

Refrain 2 Fines amouretes ai trovées!(vdB 750)

Mo 5, 148 shares its refrain vdB 750, "I have found true love," with another motet (labeled motet 2 in Table 5), but no extant chansons.[13]

---

11 The three-voice musical context for refrain vdB 532 in each motet is not particularly revealing because the refrain creates some dissonance with either the tenor or the other upper voice in all three motets, perhaps a bit more pronounced in **Mo** 101 than in **Mo** 80 or 148.

12 The triplum of **Mo** 5, 80 also features a male speaker, who in this case departs to get away from slanderers.

13 The refrain survives with a different melody in **Mo** 5, 162, fol. 213v, labeled motet 3 in Table 5.

98 Malmariée *Motet Refrains within an Intertextual Nexus*

The refrain occurs in the motetus of the second motet (transmitted as a double motet in **Mo** 5, 97 and as a two-voice motet in **W2** and **N(mo)**), *Renvoisiement irai a la bele, que j'aim tant* (548)/*D'Amours sunt en grant esmai* (547)/ET SUPER (M66).[14]

Motetus
D'Amours sunt en grant esmai,
tel les ont esprovees,
et mult les ont blasmees;
mes onques ne les blasmai,
car vers moi se sunt provees
meius qu'envers eus. Bien le sai:
Fines amouretes ai trouvees.

(Love is in great trouble these days: some have tested him and heaped blame on him; but I never blamed him, for he has proven himself better toward me than toward them. I know it well: *I have found true love.*)

Here a male speaks of Love personified being in trouble because those who fail in love blame him. But the male himself feels favored by Love, and accordingly declares, "I have found true love!" At the very least, his positive words suggest that he has found a woman worthy of his attention, and at best that she reciprocates his love. When wife 2 utters the same words in **Mo** 5, 148, she follows them with "and I will keep watch over it" (see Chapter 2). That is, this *malmariée* clearly announces her intention to be vigilant in retaining her love object, expecting that her love will be reciprocated. Her viewpoint contrasts with the male's in the *grand chant courtois* tradition, whose primary action is to express his yearning for reciprocal love. Thus the refrain's context in **Mo** 5, 148 not only switches its voice from male to female, but also reveals a more determined female character in matters of love.

As shown in Example 6, the refrain is pitched at C in **Mo** 5, 148 (motet 1), whereas in motet 2, it appears at C in **W2**, but a fourth higher in **N(mo)** and **Mo** 5, 97. We return shortly to the possible significance of this pitch placement.

Refrain 3 Pleüst a Dieu que chascune de nous tenist la pieau de son mari jalous **(vdB1489)**

The lines labeled refrain 3 in both upper voices appear only in this motet. Its sentiment "May it please God that each of us have the skin of

---

14 **Mo** 5, 97 takes over the two-voice framework of **W2** and **N** largely intact.

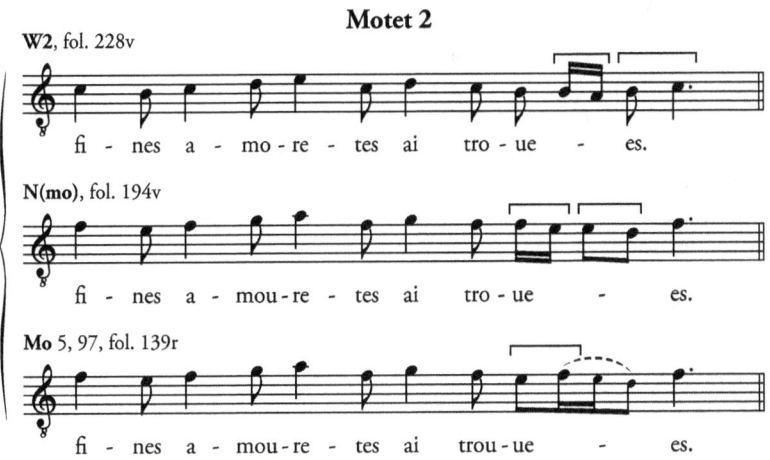

Example 6 Transmission of refrain vdB 750 melody

her jealous husband," spoken by wife 3 in the triplum and by the sole speaker in the motetus, suggests that these discontented women speak out in a spirit of solidarity.

Refrain 4 Toz li cuers me rit de joie (vdB 1781)

"My whole heart laughs with joy" has a rich history as refrain in both literary and musical contexts. We begin with *L'Art d'amours*, the thirteenth-century French translation and commentary on Ovid's *Ars amatoria*, which alternates translation with passages of gloss that are in turn "augmented with a range of citations and allusions, including French and Latin proverbs, references to French poetry and romance, one *pastourelle*, two rondeaux, six separate strophes from six different songs, and over sixty refrains."[15] Among the refrains in *L'Art d'amours* is vdB 1781: *Tout le cuer me rit de joie, quant (je) la voi* (when I see her). This same text version appears in two *chansons avec des refrains*,

---

15 Butterfield, *Poetry and Music*, 256. See also Saltzstein, "Ovid and the Thirteenth-Century Motet," 351–72.

both attributed to trouvères from Arras: *Penser ne doit vilanie* by Jehan Erart (ca. 1200/10–1258/9, labeled *chanson avec des refrains 1* in Table 5) and *Li beaus tens d'esté* by Colart le Boutellier (fl. 1240–60) (labeled *chanson avec des refrains 2* in Table 5). Both are transmitted without music in trouvère MS **M** (copied after 1253, probably 1260s or 1270s in Artois, possibly in Arras); other sources of one or the other chanson are dated 1270–80 and connected to Picardy-Artois, Artois, or specifically Arras.[16] The refrain captures the male speaker's joy at seeing his loved one. The wording in **Mo** 5, 148 is the same, except that *la* appears in place of *le*, as the third wife, speaking of her sweetheart, utters the refrain: *Touz li cuers me rit de joie quant le voi* (when I see him). The dating of the relevant sources allows that the creator of **Mo** 5, 148 may have known the refrain from the secular song tradition in which a man delights in the sight of the woman, and changed its personal pronoun object to accommodate the *malmariée* who experiences joy at the sight of her lover.

But our picture is complicated by the fact that vdB 1781 is also found in *La Court de Paradis*, written at the end of the thirteenth century. In the *Paradis* version of refrain vdB 1781, *dieu* appears in place of *le* or *la*: *Touz li cuer me rit de joie quant dieu voi* According to Sylvia Huot, scholars assume that the *Paradis* author took this and other secular refrains and adapted them for a devotional application.[17] One of the three *Paradis* manuscripts, **Pa 25532** (dated to the end of the thirteenth century, probably from St-Médard de Soissons in northern France), notates the refrain, revealing a melodic profile that largely agrees with what is found in **Mo** 5, 148 (motet 1), though pitched a fourth lower and with slightly less ornamentation (see Example 7).[18]

Notably, another motet from fascicle 5 of **Mo** also figures in the refrain transmission: **Mo** 5, 115, *Tant me fait a vos penser* (17)/*Tout li cuers me rit de joie* (18)/*OMNES* (M1) (labeled motet 2 in Example 7 and in Table 5), presents the refrain beginning *tout li cuers me rit de joie* (text and music) at the same pitch level as in **Mo** 5, 148, but with a slightly varied onset gesture (C B C rather than D C B C) in order to

---

16 *Penser ne doit vilanie* appears in MSS **KMN(tr)PTX**. *Li beaus tens d'esté* appears in trouvère MSS **M** and **a**. Of *Penser ne doit vilanie*'s six sources, four (**KN(tr)PX**) attribute it to Jehan Erart, one (**M**) to Guiot de Dijon (fl. 1215–25, a Burgundian trouvère), and one (**T**) to Andrieu Contredit (ca. 1200–48, a trouvère from Arras).
17 She considers the *Paradis* "an allegorical—and witty—use of popular refrains" that invests them with new meaning. Huot, *Allegorical Play*, 82.
18 The other two manuscripts are **Pa 837**, fol. 59va (end of the thirteenth century, after 1276); and **Pa 1802**, fol. 104r (fourteenth century).

Motet 1

Mo 5, 148, fols. 200v–201r

[PORTARE]

Motet 2

Mo 5, 115, fols. 157v–158v, Ba no. 91, fol. 57rb

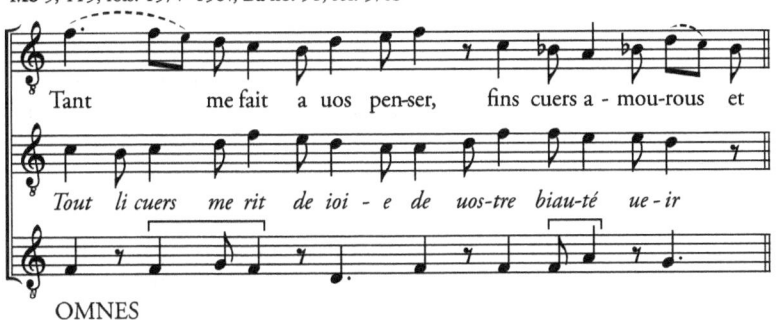

OMNES

Court de Paradis

Pa 25532, fol. 334va

Example 7 Transmission of refrain vdB 1781 melody

create consonance with the different tenor. Its male speaker concludes differently: *de vostre biauté veir* (my whole heart laughs with joy when I see your beauty).[19] The music of this textual continuation also differs from the refrain's continuation in the *Paradis* and in **Mo** 5, 148. Based on this concordance picture, one can speculate on a possible scenario for the refrain's appearance in **Mo** 5, 148. In the chanson tradition, the

---

19 **Mo** 5, 115 has a concordance in **Ba**, fol. 57rb.

refrain may have been sung to the slightly less ornamented melody that survives in the *Paradis* manuscript **Pa 25532**. The creator of **Mo** 5, 148 may have known the refrain melody from the chanson tradition or from the *Paradis*, as well as from **Mo** 5, 115. **Mo** 5, 148 could have begun the refrain as notated in **Mo** 5, 115, but then for its continuation on the words *quant le/la/Dieu voi* relied on the text and music from the monophonic tradition, as transmitted in one of two chansons or the *Paradis,* all of which have surviving sources linked to Artois or another northern French locale.[20]

Looking at the whole, it becomes apparent that the creator of **Mo** 5, 148 strategically positioned the four refrains to create a highly symmetrical structure. As shown in Example 4, the tenor fragment is stated four and a half times. A full tenor statement lasts 14 perfections and its rhythmic profile remains intact on each repetition. All four refrains sound in the triplum (their entrances are marked in Example 4 above the tenor staves), while refrain 3 (vdB 1489) sounds in the motetus as well (its entrance is marked below the tenor staff). In relationship to the tenor's statements of 14, 14, 14, 14, and 7 perfections, the triplum refrains enter in an alternating pattern of 14, 13, 14, and 13 perfections, that is, refrain 1 appears after the initial 14 perfections, refrain 2 after the next 13 perfections, and so on.[21] The motet creator also cleverly positions the refrain proper to this motet, *Pleust a Dieu* (refrain 3), in the motetus to create a counterpoint with the final triplum refrain.

In view of this careful construction, we speculate on how its creator may have proceeded with the whole. As argued above, other **Mo** 5 motets probably figured prominently in **Mo** 5, 148's design, perhaps in the following way. Its creator transposed the *PORTARE* tenor to accommodate refrains 1 (vdB 532) and 4 (vdB 1781) at their notated pitch level in **Mo** 5, 80/101 and 115, respectively; using *PORTARE* at its usual notational level would have created a plethora of open-fourth sonorities between it and these two refrains. In turn, it was then necessary to notate refrain 2 (vdB 750) at the C level to suit the *PORTARE* transposition. As support for this speculation, Example 8 shows vdB 750 as it appears in **Mo** 5, 148 at its C level, but also at the higher F level, which sounds open-fourth sonorities on perfections 1 and 3 in

---

20 Notably, based on her study of the concordance picture for all the interpolated refrains in **Pa 25532**, Anne Ibos-Augé argues the reverse: she concludes the *Paradis* creator was adapting from **Mo** 5, 148; "Les Refrains de la 'Court de Paradis,'" 255–56.

21 While the first refrain enters at the beginning of the second tenor statement, the others begin over the final or penultimate note of the tenor statement.

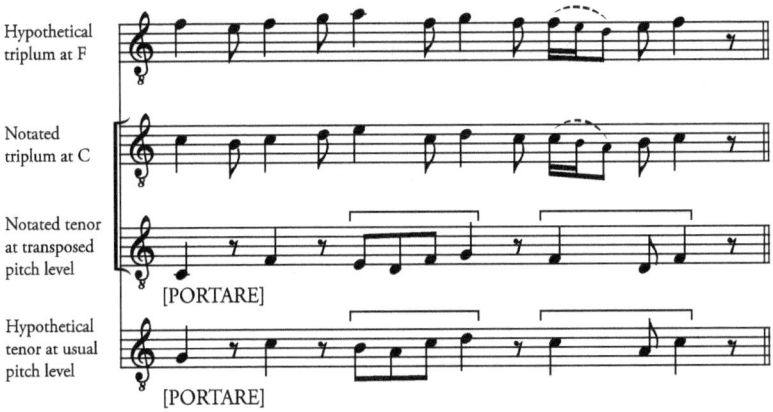

Example 8 Refrain vdB 750 and tenor *PORTARE*: hypothetical and notated pitch in **Mo** 5, 148

relationship to the transposed tenor, while the penultimate E against tenor D creates a striking dissonance that the creator may have wanted to avoid.[22] Whether the motet creator might have known vdB 750 at the F level from **N(mo)** or **Mo** 5, 97 and transposed it down to C, or from **W2**, where it was already at the C level, cannot be determined from the available evidence. As discussed earlier, the transmission of this particular refrain in **Mo** 5, 148 lends support to the idea of Mo's connection to **N(mo)** and **W2**, but no more specific pathway comes to light through the present study.

I want to reflect momentarily on the artistic "product" of this highly constructed example. The collage-like triplum text makes sense as a whole, as the three unhappy wives present the refrains in turn. The three wives are also mentioned in the motetus, but only one speaks. The triplum refrains are audible, particularly at their outset, because the motetus doubles their pitches; while the words might be somewhat obscured, the melodies certainly are not. In general, this motet is characterized by consecutive parallel octave and fifth movement between the outermost sounding voices. The combination of the three refrains shared with other sources and the tenor fragment *PORTARE* creates these parallels; the fourth so-called refrain, which appears to have been newly composed for this motet, does not have the same

---

22 Should vdB 750 have entered the picture earlier, with the creator of **Mo** 5, 148 considering it at the F level in relationship to *PORTARE* at its usually notated position, harsh minor seventh dissonances would have resulted, as shown in Example 8.

high degree of parallelism with the tenor.²³ Yet the opening fourteen perfections, before the refrains enter, also reveal a significant level of parallelisms, suggesting that the composer might have adopted the "harmonic sound" associated with the refrain contexts as the sound of the motet as a whole.²⁴

In addition to their likely role in shaping the motet's musical sound, the refrains uttered by the *malmariées*, three of which were spoken by males in other sources, dominate this motet. They reveal her agency and resolve in matters of love, contrasting with, and perhaps parodying, the inactivity of the males who utter them in other contexts. Finally, as discussed in Chapter 2, the combined effect of the women's direct complaints against their husbands, even wishing that the husbands die, offers a less than subtle parody of Mary, who was assumed into Heaven to become the devoted Bride of Christ.

Mo 2, 23 *Dame que j'aim et desir/Amors vaint tot fors/Au tans d'esté/***ET GAUDEBIT** **and Mo 5, 142** *Nus ne set les biens d'amors/Ja dieus ne me doinst corage/***PORTARE**

As shown in Table 6 (Appendix A), the four-voice *malmariée* motet **Mo 2, 23** on *ET GAUDEBIT*, which is often cited in the literature for its *cento* tendencies, contains six refrains. Five of the six survive only in motets, and the sixth (vdB 900) in motets and a chanson.²⁵ The fol-

---

23 A comment about the motet's transmission in **Mo** is in order vis-à-vis this newly composed refrain: While the refrain appears in full at its first appearance in the triplum, its return in the motetus is missing music notation for its first several words, *Pleüst a Dieu, que chascu-*, which fall at the end of the second of two incomplete staves. Why the music notator left the two staves incomplete cannot be determined from the available evidence.

24 Those fourteen perfections constitute the first tenor statement, with the first refrain appearing immediately after in the triplum over a new tenor statement. Though not isomelic in a strict sense, the overall relationship between these two statements is fairly intact, with the first statement emulating in its combined upper voices the highest pitches of the triplum refrain.

25 Mark Everist, "The Refrain Cento: Myth or Motet?" *Journal of the Royal Music Association* 114 (1989): 164–88, at 181, note 53. See also Everist, *French Motets in the Thirteenth Century*, 119, note 34. In his 1989 article, Everist observed that only three of the seven refrains so designated by Doss-Quinby and Gennrich (and more equivocally by Tischler) can be found in other sources, and thus he problematized the designation of this motet as a *refrain cento*. The most up-to-date work on this motet is available through the online data base *Refrains*, which now identifies six refrains, of which three reveal intertextuality with other motets.

lowing discussion does not address the three refrains transmitted only within **Mo** 2, 23 and its concordances, but concentrates instead on its three refrains shared with other motets: vdB 587 and 900, which appear within the *malmariée* motet **Mo** 5, 142 on *PORTARE* (900 is also found in a chanson), and vdB 664, found in two other motets in **Mo**, fascicle 5.

Refrain vdB 587, *Doleroz mari, vous ne savrés hui qui amiete je sui,* opens **Mo** 2, 23 (motet 1), whereas it serves as the closing refrain of the motetus in **Mo** 5, 142 (motet 2), where its first two words are not "sorrowful husband" but instead "Fie, villain with the madly contorted face," as discussed in Chapter 2. As shown in Example 9, the two motets set the different words of the refrain opening with what may loosely be interpreted as two shared gestures (circled), while the second halves share the same intervals and rhythm, but with the pitch level shifted up a second in **Mo** 5, 142. If the creator of **Mo** 5, 142 had presented the second half of the refrain at the same pitch level as in **Mo** 2, 23 and its concordances,[26] consecutive dissonances would have resulted at the beginning of the four perfections that set the words *vous ne sarés hui qui a-* (see the tenor *PORTARE* in Example 10 in relationship to the **Mo** 2, 23 triplum).

The second shared refrain vdB 900, *Ja Dex ne mi doint corage d'amer mon mari tant conme j'aie ami,* opens the motetus of **Mo** 5, 142 (motet 2), in this case with both the music and text largely unchanged from what appears in the triplum of **Mo** 2, 23 (motet 1), though pitched up a fifth (see Example 11). Again, the transposition may reflect the fact that the tenor *PORTARE* would have created some less satisfactory sonorities with the refrain at the lower C pitch level (see the tenor *PORTARE* in Example 11 in relationship to the **Mo** 2, 23 triplum, particularly the high number of vertical fourths that result). But one spot (boxed) reveals a different melodic contour than in **Mo** 2, 23. On the other hand, as shown in Example 11, **Mo** 2, 23's concordances that transmit music (**Ba** and **LoV**) share **Mo** 5, 142's contour at this spot. The refrain's meaning remains intact between the two *malmariée* motets.

---

26 **Mo** 2, 23, in four voices, is concordant with **Bes**, no. 47, which does not transmit music. A three-voice concordance is found in **Ba**, fol. 5v and **LoV**, fol. 164v; in their transmission of refrain 587, **Mo** and **Ba** are exactly the same, while **LoV** has two relatively minor variants.

Example 9 Transmission of refrain vdB 587 melody in **Mo 2, 23** and **Mo 5, 142**

Motet 1

Mo 2, 23, fol. 33vb triplum

Motet 2

Mo 5, 142, fol. 194r motetus and tenor

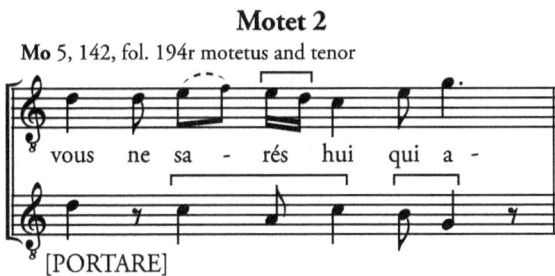

Example 10 Second half of refrain vdB 587 in **Mo** 2, 23 versus in **Mo** 5, 142 over tenor *PORTARE*

Refrain 900 also survives in a *chanson avec des refrains*, *Se felon et losengier*, in trouvère sources **KN(trv)PX** (all copied 1270–80 in the Picardy-Artois region) and **R(trv)** (fr. 1591) from the first quarter of the fourteenth century, but without music.[27] The male speaker of the chanson, concerned with slanderers and their harmful effects, ends the final verse with a *malmariée* uttering vdB 900: "May God never give me the desire to love my husband as long as I have a lover."

Based on this source profile, the creator of **Mo** 5, 142 may have known its opening refrain vdB 900 from the chanson as well as the other *malmariée* motet, though not necessarily from its appearance in **Mo** 2, 23. Regardless, both of **Mo** 5, 142's refrain citations put it into a nexus with another *malmariée* motet. As discussed in Chapter 2, the interaction between the two *malmariée* motets extends beyond their sharing of two refrains; in both, the *malmariée* in one voice sounds against a male idealizing love in another. Two interpretations of this juxtaposition seem possible: the woman who actively pursues the fulfillment of her desires can parody the male's inactivity, or her openness to adultery can empower the male who fantasizes about love. In either

---

27 For MS **R(trv)**, see Christopher Callahan, "Thibaut de Champagne and Disputed Attributions: The Case of MSS Bern, Burgerbibliothek 389 (C) and Paris, BnF fr. 1591(R)," *Textual Cultures* 5/1 (Spring 2010): 111–32. Of the chanson's five sources, three attribute it to Philippe Paon and one to Jeannot Paon, both of whom we know almost nothing about. The later MS **R(trv)** does not offer an attribution.

Example 11 Transmission of refrain vdB 900 in **Mo** 2, 23 and **Mo** 5, 142

case, the two motets' shared features indicate that modeling may have been in play, despite the fact that they are based on different tenors.

Mo 2, 23 connects with another Montpellier motet in fascicle 5, **Mo** 5, 106, *Quant la froidor trait a fin* (226)/*L'autrier chevauchoie deles un vergier* (227)/*Nostrum* (M14) (labeled motet 2 in Table 6) through their shared transmission of a different refrain, vdB 664, within their respective triplum voices. In **Mo** 2, 23, the refrain appears within a *malmariée* text, while in **Mo** 5, 106 the context is a *pastourelle*, and thus we witness an interplay of song types *across* motets. In **Mo** 2, 23, lines 37–38, the discontented wife, speaking of her lover, utters: *En non Diu, amors me tienent, ja n'en garirai.* (In the name of God, love has me in his grip and never will I be cured.) As Example 12 shows, **Mo** 5, 106, lines 14–16, present the exact same music for the refrain at the same pitch level as in **Mo** 2, 23. The refrain in **Mo** 5, 106 is voiced by a love-besotted shepherdess as she rejects the male narrator who happens upon her and attempts to seduce her. She responds to him: *J'ai ami cointe et gai* (I have a charming, gay sweetheart), followed by vdB 664. But the shepherdess's final refrain words are *ja n'en partirai* instead of *ja n'en garirai* (In the name of God, love has me in his grip and I shall never *leave him*). Several interrelated questions arise: Is the antecedent for *en* "love" or "sweetheart"? Is this a deliberate word substitution, or might the creator or copier of **Mo** 5, 106 have unintentionally used *partirai* instead of *garirai*, given that *partirai* is the final word of the immediately following, final refrain in **Mo** 2, 23, vdB 748,

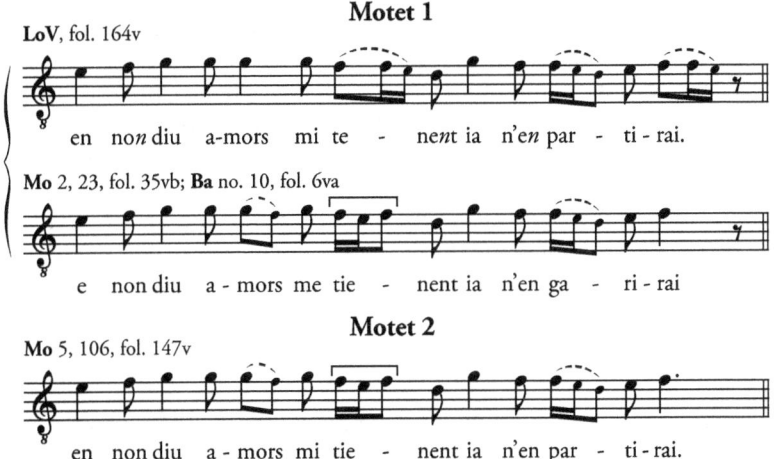

Example 12 Transmission of refrain vdB 664 in **Mo** 2, 23 and **Mo** 5, 106

Fines amouretes ai et bel ami joli, dont ja ne partirai? In other words, was this an unintentional textual conflation? Looking further, of **Mo** 2, 23's two concordances that transmit music (see Example 12), **Ba** also transmits *garirai*, whereas **LoV**, a slightly later source, ca. 1300, uses *partirai*, the ending word in **Mo** 5, 106. Finally, two other extant motets, labeled motets 3 and 4 in Table 6, transmit vdB 664 with the final word *partirai*. Whereas motet 4 appears in the early fourteenth-century **Douce 308**, motet 3 (**Mo** 5, 108) appears within the same fascicle as **Mo** 5, 106. At the very least, these additional two motets indicate a common transmission of the refrain with *partirai*. In view of all these factors, it seems reasonable to believe that **Mo** 5, 106 could relate directly to **Mo** 2, 23.[28]

These three *malmariée* motets on the tenor *PORTARE* (**Mo** 6, 233; **Mo** 5, 148; and **Mo** 5, 142) strongly suggest borrowing among motets, even if the motet creators may also have known other refrain sources such as lyric songs and narrative poems. Given that the *PORTARE* motets are newly composed, their creators could design their works to draw attention to their borrowed refrains, such as in the highly structured **Mo** 5, 148. Significantly, that motet's refrains vdB 532, 750, and 1781 appear in other motets within fascicle 5 of Montpellier, spoken by a male, and may well have been adapted from those motets into the female voice of **Mo** 5, 148. When listeners familiar with the refrains in male voices heard them within the *malmariées'* declarations of action, they may have reflected on the different obstacles encountered by men and women in matters of love.

Mo 5, 142 relates specifically to another *malmariée* motet, the *cento* **Mo** 2, 23 or its concordances, through two shared refrains, vdB 587 and 900. **Mo** 2, 23 in turn connects to another motet within fascicle 5, **Mo** 5, 106 through refrain vdB 664. Unlike **Mo** 5, 148, whose refrains voiced by an unhappily married woman are spoken in other motets by a male in the *grand chant courtois* tradition, the refrain shared by **Mo** 2, 23 and **Mo** 5, 106 remains in a female voice: a *malmariée* versus a shepherdess. For both women, the refrain conveys her defiance, signaling that she does not accept the constraints of marriage nor the amorous advances of an unwanted suitor.

The two-voice *malmariée* motet on *PORTARE*, **Mo** 6, 233, offers yet another glimpse into intertextuality among motets through its shared

---

28 The creator of **Mo** 5, 106 may also have known the refrain text from motet 3, **Mo** 5, 108, where a male proclaims that he will never leave his sought-after loved one. **Mo** 5, 108 reverses the two halves of the textual refrain and provides different music from what is found in motets 1 and 2. The refrain ends with *partirai*. Table 6 refers to motet 4 in **Douce 308**, which contains a seven-line text that is framed by the two halves of the refrain: line 1 = first half, line 7 = second half. This appearance of the refrain ends in *partirai* as well. The *Refrain* database calls the parent work *An! an! an! Dieus, Amours mi tiennent.*

refrain vdB 1691 with the two-voice motet *Cele m'a s'amour/ALLE-LUIA.HODIE MARIA VIRGO CELOS ASCENDIT.* Appearing on consecutive folios within manuscript **N(mo)**, both motets use tenors associated with the Assumption and both parody its liturgical message: Mary as devoted Bride of Christ. Though the available evidence precludes a firm conclusion on the direction of borrowing, the overt refrain sharing is striking in these two Assumption-related motets, particularly in view of the importance of the Assumption feast in the locale where **N(mo)** was produced. The conclusion will reflect further on MS **N(mo)** and what contributions this study of the *malmariée* corpus can make to our understanding of manuscript relationships involving **N(mo)**.

Mo 2, 30 *Cest quadruble sans reison* (798)/*Voz n'i dormirés ja mais* (799)/*Biaus cuers renvoisiés et douz* (800)/*FIAT*

As argued in Chapter 3, **Mo** 2, 30 contains two refrains in its triplum and motetus (vdB 1867 and 217, respectively) that it probably drew from *L'art d'amours*, a conjecture supported by the fact that the motet acknowledges and adapts the dialogic nature of the particular *L'art d'amours* gloss passage that contains these two refrains. The respective dating allows this directional borrowing: the text refrains appear in Book 2 of the treatise, dated to the first third of the century, whereas **Mo** fascicle 2 is believed to have been copied in the late 1270s or 1280s.[29] The meaning of the two refrains shared with *L'art d'amours* remains the same in both contexts: a man asks when a woman will sleep with him, and she rejects him.

The quadruplum contains a third refrain, vdB 1540 *Puis que bele dame m'aime, je ne demant plus* (When such a fair lady loves me, I ask for nothing more), which it shares with two other motets preserved in **Mo**, both on a different tenor, *FLOS FILIUS EIUS* (see Table 7 (Appendix A)). **Mo** 2, 30 is motet 1 (concordance in **Cl**), while motet 2 survives in **Mo** 2, 22 in four voices (concordance in **Cl**) and in **Mo** 5, 145 in three voices (concordance in **Ba**). Motet 3 on the other hand survives as a two-voice motet in both **Mo** 6, 231 and **N(mo)**. The refrain's melodic transmission in these various sources is exact, except for a slight variant in the final words *demant plus*, whose degree of significance is unclear.[30]

How might **Mo** 2, 30 (motet 1) have come into being as a four-voice French motet with three refrains? As discussed in Chapter 3, its creator

---

29 The extant manuscripts of the treatise are not revealing, because all four date to the fifteenth century.
30 Motet 1 in **Mo** uses ending 1, but its concordance in **Cl** uses ending 2. All sources of motet 2 (three- or four-voice) share ending 1. Motet 3 in **N(mo)** uses ending 2, and in **Mo** a hybrid of endings 1 and 2.

probably wrote a French contrafact of a Latin double motet in **Ba**, making the two upper voices begin by proclaiming simultaneously the first line of refrains 1867 and 217, respectively (from *L'art d'amours*), and end with the second and third lines of the refrains, again simultaneously. Notably, **Mo** 2, 22 (motet 2), also in four voices, concludes with a tour-de-force simultaneous utterance of *three* refrains, with refrain vdB 1540 in its quadruplum. Might the creator of motet 1, attracted to the simultaneous concluding utterance of three refrains in motet 2, have decided to emulate that ending by adding its own quadruplum whose final phrase also incorporates the text and music of vdB 1540?

Quadruplum Mo 2, 30
Cest quadruble sans reison
n'ai pas fete en tel seison,
qu'oisel chanter n'ose.
Quar se je repose
de fere chançon,
s'amor, qui arose
mon cuer environ,
ne perdra grant souprison.
Se ai esté lonc tens
en sa prison
et en atent guerredon,
biaus sui de sens:
Quant si bele dame m'aime,   vdB 1540
je ne demant plus.

Quadruplum Mo 2, 22
Par un matinet l'autrier
oï chanter un fou berchier,
(s'en fui esmeü,)
qui se vantoit, qu'il ot geü tout nu
entre les deus bras s'amie.
Il se vantoit de folie,
car tele amour est vilaine.
Mes j'aim certes plus loiaument que nus:
Puisque bele dame m'aime,   vdB 1540
je ne demant plus.

The refrain's identity is intact except for the one substitution, *quant si* versus *puisque*. In both contexts, the male speaker defends his elevated sort of love: in **Mo** 2, 22, in comparison to a shepherd's base coupling with his sweetheart, and in **Mo** 2, 30, within an assertion that he is in his right senses (*biaus sui de sens*). This correspondence of meaning supports the idea of modeling between the two motets. One notes that the vertical relationship among the lower three voices of **Mo** 2, 30 is already dissonant at *vous trovai/quant dormirai*, but increases with the addition of *Quant si bele* in the quadruplum. Given that the vertical relationship among the voices in motet 2 when the refrains sound together is also not optimum, the modeling could have been reversed, with motet 2 mimicking the ending in motet 1.

How motet 3 (**Mo** 6, 231) fits into the picture is unclear, though the fact that it uses the same tenor as motet 2, as well as the same refrain, argues for a relationship between those two. Motet 3 separates the two phrases of the refrain to form a frame for the motetus voice, which is the technique used in motet 1 for the other two refrains, but not for vdB 1540:

> *Puisque bele dame m'eime,*
> destourber ne m'i doit nus;
> quar iere si loiaus drus,
> que je n'iere ja tenus
> pour faus amans ne vantanz.
> Ja li mesdisant
> N'en seront joiant,
> car nul mal ne vois querant;
> mes qu'ami me cleime,
> *je ne demant plus.*

Here, as in the other two motets within this nexus, the male speaker argues for the unimpeachable nature of his love.

We turn to the possible meanings generated when **Mo** 2, 30's quadruplum, which includes refrain vdB 1540, interacts with the paired motetus and triplum texts, which mimic a dialogue between a man and woman. As discussed in Chapter 3, the woman in the triplum who refuses the sexual overtures of the male in the motetus could be interpreted as a *malmariée*. The idea of a male pressing a woman for sex would have contrasted with the quaduplum refrain vdB 1540 spoken by a male: *when such a fair lady loves me, I ask for nothing more*. While the male in the motetus engages the women, the male in the quaduplum waits, claiming that his sort of distant love is admirable. In comparing the three speakers, a listener would note that the woman in the triplum seems to retain the upper hand. If a double parody of male behaviors was intended, we witness a more sophisticated treatment of the *malmariée topos* than in many examples within the corpus. We also recall that, because **Mo** 2, 30 probably began as a contrafact of a double Latin motet to which it added a fourth voice, none of its voices enters into dialogue with the Latin tenor *FIAT*, also making it stand out within this oeuvre.

Finally, it is of note that **N(mo)** comes into play in the intertextual use of refrain vdB 1540 (see motet 3 in Table 7), as it did for the transmission and intertextuality of the *PORTARE* motets and their refrains.

Conclusion

Contents

The issues of mutual consent and marital debt raised at the beginning of this study permeate this motet corpus. Although complaints about an arranged marriage surface in only three examples, the nuance and detail provided lend a sense of reality to the complaints: one woman rants against a mother who knew she was in love with someone else; one admits she knew in advance that she would cuckold her husband; one expresses doubt on how to behave, given that she finds her coupling with an older man untenable. On the marital debt itself, the *malmariées* in the motet corpus generally admit that they cannot escape it. A majority nonetheless are open to having a lover. Some keep their extramarital alliances from the husband; others suggest that they rub it in the husband's face, one even telling him he can exact his will *after* she exercises hers with her lover. Even if the *malmariées*' response to marital constraints were sometimes carried out more in their imagination than in fact, their utterances reflect the realities of marriage for some women in the thirteenth century.

In its examination of how the motet of this period engages with the topos of the unhappily married woman, this study has repeatedly used the word "play," an apt characterization following from Sylvia Huot's use of the word in her seminal study, *Allegorical Play in the Old French Motet*. Because the genre inherently takes as its foundation a liturgical chant, listeners would have come to expect that a *malmariée* text interacts in some way with the spiritual sentiment expressed in the chant-carrying tenor. "Play" captures the sense of creativity and humor that arises from the sounding interaction of a divine individual, most often Christ or Mary, and the down-to-earth wife or prospective wife. We hear her speak, either directly or through a male narrator, as she brings to light the challenges experienced by a woman in a marital context. Her tone may be sad, mocking, or defiant.

DOI: 10.4324/9781003335405-10

Conclusion 115

When she expresses a defiant wish to fulfill her own desires, there results a parodic play with liturgical tenors that resonate a message of Christian love and devotion to others: specifically, *IMMOLATUS* (**Mo** 6, 203 and **Mo** 6, 180), which addresses Christ's sacrificial act, and two tenors taken from the Assumption liturgy that focus on Mary's selfless devotion to Christ, particularly as his heavenly Bride— *PORTARE* (**Mo** 6, 233, **Mo** 5, 142, **Mo** 5, 148) and *VERITATEM* (**Mo** 5, 156, **Mo** 5, 169).

At other times, the *malmariée*'s expressed wish to refuse marriage and seek a different sort of love may enter into an allegorical play with a tenor. In the context of two Pentecost tenors, *AMORIS* (EM 310) and *DOCEBIT* (**Mo** 6, 243), which respectively convey the inspirational and comforting love of the Holy Spirit, her wish for a different sort of love may be interpreted allegorically as her desire for a religious profession.

Overall, the *malmariée* incipits are derived largely from the Easter-Ascension-Pentecost liturgies (five total) or the feast of the Assumption (five total). Outside of those just mentioned, other liturgical tenors in this corpus appear in only one surviving motet and thereby preclude making any generalizations about their interpretive treatment. Nonetheless, as shown in column 7 in Table 1, the interaction between the *malmariée* and Latin tenors as a whole reveals more parodic than allegorical play (the table puts into parentheses any additional reading that results from the interaction of a voice other than the *malmariée* with the tenor). This observation holds even if we reduce the parodic numbers by one to account for the likely direct borrowing between **Mo** 2, 23 and **Mo** 5, 142. **Mo** 7, 276 even suggests a tantalizing possibility that parody could be double-barreled: the unhappily married man in the motetus can perhaps be read as a parody of a complaining, unhappily married woman, as well as a parody of Christ's suffering in the underlying tenor.

Just as "play" appropriately applies to the interaction between the *malmariée* voice and liturgical tenor, it also describes well the interactions between the *malmariée* topos and subtypes of the chanson, which could occur within the motet's *malmariée* voice, between that voice and another upper voice, or through the motet's intertextual use of a refrain known from other sources. Most prominent intergeneric plays are with the *pastourelle* and the *grand chant courtois*.

A motet may use *pastourelle* elements, in particular the encounter framework, within its *malmariée* text. A listener's expectations of a narrator coming upon a seemingly unprotected shepherdess are thwarted when he instead encounters a defiant *malmariée*. After that initial disconnect, the listener might reflect on the fact that the shepherdess who refuses the narrator's advances ultimately shares the *malmariée*'s same self-assertive trait. Combining the two topoi within the *malmariée* text occurs in **Mo** 6, 203, **Mo** 6, 233, and **Mo** 5, 148. Interaction between the *malmariée* topos and the *pastourelle* can also result when a motet uses a refrain known from a *chanson* that uses an encounter frame. **Mo** 6, 203, EM 389, and **Mo** 8, 325 employ intergeneric play of this sort. The first two cases foreground and intensify the married woman's perspective in comparison to that of the narrator in the chanson who relates her words. The third case changes the perspective entirely: the speaker who fears being discovered switches from the chanson's male predator intending to seduce a shepherdess to the motet's *malmariée* determined to meet up with her willing lover. The "play" in this case might lead a listener who knows the chanson to reflect on the fact that both individuals transgress societal norms.

When play occurs between the *grand chant courtois* and *malmariée* topoi, the modus operandi seems to be contrasting the apparently empowered *malmariée*, who acts on her desires, with the male of the *grand chant courtois*, who does not act, but professes an idealized love. The contrast may have been interpreted as parody of the male, though the juxtaposition of these two topoi may also have been viewed as empowering the male: the seemingly unattainable woman *becomes* attainable when she expresses a desire for a lover. Such a gendered contrast may occur between the *malmariée* text and another upper voice, as in **Mo** 2, 23, **Mo** 5, 142, and **Mo** 7, 271. But motets can also bring the two topoi into play by using refrains that appear in other sources, including motets. For example, three of **Mo** 5, 148's refrains spoken by an unhappily married woman are presented by a male in the *grand chant courtois* tradition in other fascicle 5 motets, while a refrain shared by **Mo** 2, 23 and **Mo** 5, 106 remains in a female voice: a *malmariée* versus a shepherdess. A listener who knows both motet contexts might reflect on a given refrain's blatant change of gender perspective and meaning in **Mo** 5, 148, while, in the case of the refrain shared by **Mo** 2, 23 and **Mo** 5, 106, its more nuanced transformation.

This repertory thus offers us an entrée into how thirteenth-century motet creators and their audiences may have viewed women's and men's roles in matters of love, and particularly in the context of marriage. A direct reading of the *malmariée*'s utterances might view her as capable of self-determination. But in her parodic relationship with the divine Christ or Mary of the tenor, the irony might be read as directed at her, mocking her pretentious stance. She may seem favorably empowered in relationship to the acquiescent male of the *grand chant courtois* with whom she is pitted in intergeneric play. Likewise, through a *malmariée* motet's interplay with the *pastourelle* topos, a listener might reflect

Conclusion

on the perceived self-confidence of both the married woman and the shepherdess. Other motets can lead us to reflect on her transgressive adultery instead of the husband's abusive treatment of her. In short, although the *malmariée* comes across in some instances as a stock character whose predictable attributes and behavior can be mocked, the skillful play of these motets complicates that simple view. The corpus allows that the unhappily married woman can be insightful about her rights as a human being, even as she remains trapped in a loveless marriage. Her willingness to commit adultery is undeniable, even if more fantasized than real. Exposing these views in what are sometimes tour-de-force interactions among a motet's voices or between a motet and other sources attracted motet creators in the thirteenth century.

Transmission and Intertextuality

This study noted at the outset that a corpus of *chansons de femme*, typically anonymous, emanated from northern France at the time of the trouvères; as a subcategory of this lyric type, *malmariée* songs share this profile. But for the *malmariée* motet repertory, the sources primarily implicate Paris: the Parisian-produced Montpellier manuscript contains fourteen of the eighteen motets. Of the four *malmariée* motets that do not appear in **Mo**, three survive only in manuscripts produced in northern France: EM 310 (two-voice) in the Artesian **R(mo)** and **N(mo)**; EM 389 and 415 (single French text) as unica in **Douce 308** from Lorraine. The fourth motet, Turin, Biblioteca reale, varia 42 (**Tu**), f. 16 (three-voice), is also a unicum. **Tu** is dated to ca. 1300, and the orthography of the French motet texts suggests a Walloon scribe; the manuscript was housed at the Benedictine Abbey of Saint Jacques in Liège until the eighteenth century.[1]

Malmariée motet concordances and, in one case, a tenor concordance, add additional information to the transmission picture. Of the five two-voice motets in the sixth fascicle of Montpellier, two implicate the Artois region:

Mo 6, 233	concordance in Artesian **N(mo)**
Mo 6, 212	unicum, but shares its unusual tenor with another motet that survives in **ArsB**, dated to the 1270s and probably connected to the Artois region

---

1 Conveyed to me by Bradley, April 2022. See Catherine A. Bradley and Gaël Saint-Cricq, with Christopher Callahan, *An Introduction, Facsimile Reproduction, and Critical Edition of Turin, Biblioteca reale, varia 42* (Lucca: LIM Editrice, forthcoming).

118 *Conclusion*

The remaining three motets in fascicle 6 implicate Paris:

> Mo 6, 203   concordance in **W2** (mid-thirteenth century, probably Paris)
>
> Mo 6, 243   concordance in **StV** (1270–1300, Paris), whose two-voice clausula (with motetus text incipit) is believed to have drawn from the motet[2]
>
> Mo 6, 180   concordance in **F** (1240s, Paris), whose two-voice clausula is believed to have drawn from the motet

Thus, of the total eight examples transmitted with a single French text or in two voices, three survive only in northern French sources (EM 310, 389, 415), two in **Mo** 6 (233 and 212) are connected to the Artois region through a concordance or unusual shared tenor, and the remaining three in **Mo** 6 (203, 243, 180) insinuate Paris through their concordances. **Mo** 6, 203's concordance in W2, an earlier, probably Parisian source, offers a clear instance of a malmariée motet that predated the compilation of **Mo**.

Turning to the malmariée motets (three- and four-voice) in remaining fascicles of **Mo**, one finds the following transmission profile:

> Mo 2, 23   concordance in **Ba**, **Bes**, and **LoV**
>
> Mo 2, 30   concordance in **Cl** (also double Latin motet in **Ba**)
>
> Mo 5, 142   unicum
>
> Mo 5, 148   concordance in **Bes**
>
> Mo 5, 156   unicum
>
> Mo 5, 169   double Latin motet concordance in **Mo** 4, 64
>
> Mo 7, 271   concordance in **Vat. 1543**
>
> Mo 7, 276   concordance in **Hu**
>
> Mo 8, 325   unicum

Leaving aside fascicle 2 for the moment, the surviving concordances of the seven three-voice motets in fascicles 5, 7, and 8 indicate a limited circulation that does not include northern France. Three are unica, and **Mo** 5, 169 has a double Latin version in the same manuscript. Otherwise, only manuscripts **Bes**, **Vat. 1543**, and **Hu** are involved. **Mo** would have preceded **Hu**, since the latter's main corpus dates to the 1340s, for use at the Cistercian monastery in Burgos, Spain.[3] While

---

[2] The three-voice concordant motet in **Tu** (ca. 1300) would have been later than the **Mo** 6 motet.

[3] See David Catalunya, "Music, Space and Ritual in Medieval Castille, 1221–1350" (Ph.D. diss., Universität Würzburg, 2016), Chapter 4.

Bes (which transmits text incipits only) is thought to have been produced in Besançon in eastern France, its dating within the thirteenth century has not been delimited.[4] The motet fragment in **Vat. 1543** probably comes from a "motet manuscript of the French type," dated to the late thirteenth century, with notation similar to that in **Mo 7** and **8**.[5] Thus, the dating of **Bes** and **Vat. 1543** does not shed light on the likely transmission patterns for **Mo 5**, 148 and **Mo 7**, 271, respectively; nonetheless, **Bes** and **Vat. 1543**, as concordances, reveal the two motets' circulation in France.

The two four-voice motets in **Mo**, fascicle 2 have concordances with four manuscripts: **Ba**, **Bes**, **LoV**, and **Cl**. Leaving aside **LoV**, which postdates **Mo** (ca. 1300 with English mensural features), the other three sources are French, with dating that is unclear or close to **Mo**'s, obscuring the direction of transmission. The latest scholarship on **Ba**, traditionally thought to have been produced in Paris, suggests that it may be linked to southern France because of its mixture of Italian and northern French influences; though usually dated to 1275, its decorations allow for a wider consideration to the fourth quarter of the century.[6] **Bes** was probably compiled in eastern France sometime in the thirteenth century. According to Sean Curran's codicological study of **Cl**, its motet fascicle ("production unit 12") may have belonged to the earliest of three identifiable bindings probably completed before the death of Louis IX in 1270. This dating would put **Cl** slightly before **Mo**. Though Curran argues that **Cl**'s production methods do not conform to those practiced in the highly centralized book trade in Paris or even its ecclesiastical institutions and University, he does not preclude Parisian provenance.[7] In any case, the three concordances whose dating is unclear or close to **Mo 2**'s seem to be of French provenance, with **Cl** (and **Ba**) possibly Parisian; none links to northern France with certainty.

4   Information accessed on July 31, 2020, at https://portail.biblissima.fr/en/ark:/43093/mdata556c83ffdf875e56d00d40ad7defa132118d6b26.
5   Quoted from RISM, B/IV, 1.
6   **Ba** has long been considered of Parisian provenance. But that association has been questioned by Pfändtne, "Zum Enstehungsraum," 161–6. He suggests in a preliminary fashion that southern France is a more likely point of origin because of the manuscript's mixture of Italian and northern French influences.
7   Sean Curran, "Writing, Performance, and Devotion in the Thirteenth-Century Motet: The 'La Clayette' Manuscript," in *Manuscripts and Medieval Song. Inscription, Performance, Context*, ed. Helen Deeming and Elizabeth Eva Leach (Cambridge: Cambridge University Press, 2015), 193–220, at 202–4. See also Curran, "Composing a Codex: The Motets in the 'La Clayette' Manuscript," in *Medieval Music in Practice: Studies in Honor of Richard Crocker*, ed. Judith A. Peraino (Middleton, WI: American Institute of Musicology, 2013), 219–53.

120 Conclusion

Thus, of the eighteen total *malmariée* motets, five reveal strong connections to northern France: three (EM 310, 389, and 415) are transmitted only in northern sources (**N(mo)**, **R(mo)**, and **Douce 318**); **Mo** 6, 233 has a concordance in **N(mo)**; and **Mo** 6, 212, a unicum, has an unusual tenor concordance with another motet in the Artesian manuscript **ArsB**. Of the remaining twelve motets in **Mo**, three are unica; one has a double Latin motet concordance in **Mo**; four also appear in a source clearly or relatively securely tied to Paris; and four also appear in sources that postdate **Mo**, are close to its dating, or equivocally dated, of which three indicate some circulation in France, but not northern France. The unicum **Tu**, f. 16 has a connection to Liège.

The intertextual nexuses for the refrain(s) that appear in thirteen of the eighteen *malmariée* motets add some additional insight into the issue of transmission.[8] Of the eight motets that share their refrains only with other genres, seven transmit refrains with strong connection to the Artois region or other northern French locales, the eighth less definitively:

EM 310	sources produced in Arras; refrain Arras
EM 389	source produced in Lorraine; refrain Lorraine and Artois
Mo 6, 212	unicum, but shares its unusual tenor with another motet that survives in ArsB, dated to the 1270s and probably connected to the Artois region; refrain Arras
Mo 6, 203	concordance in W2 (mid-thirteenth century, probably Paris); refrains Arras and Lorraine
Mo 6, 180	concordance in F (1240s, Paris), whose two-voice clausula is believed to derive from the motet; refrain Metz
Mo 7, 271	Parisian; refrain Arras
Mo 8, 325	Parisian; refrain Arras
Mo 5, 169	Parisian; refrain—northern?

The evidence of shared refrains in this subgroup of eight motets invites a bit more speculation on the cultivation and transmission of the *malmariée* topos. The refrains that feed the motets connect to Picardy-Artois or Lorraine through a song composed by a trouvère associated

---

8   **Mo** 6, 243 and EM 415 nominally contain refrains, but do not participate in intertextual nexuses. **Mo** 5, 156, **Mo** 7, 276, and **Tu**, f. 16 do not transmit refrains.

Conclusion 121

with the area and/or a source compiled in the area. If the motet's source(s) are already associated with either area, the likelihood of the motet emanating from Artois or Lorraine seems high, which would seem to be the case for EM 310 and EM 389. **Mo** 6, 212 is a bit trickier to parse, because it survives only in **Mo**, yet shares not only a refrain with a chanson by Moniot d'Arras, but also an unusual tenor and other features of a motet found only in an Artesian source. For the motets whose own sources and concordances are central, what significance can we attach to their sharing a refrain from a song composed by a northern composer and/or transmitted in northern sources? A motet creator could presumably have known the song and incorporated its refrain into a motet without himself being associated with a northern center; or the motet could have been composed in a northern center and the compiler of **Mo** copied the motet from an available exemplar that no longer survives. Leaving aside **Mo** 5, 169, perhaps that is the most that can be speculated for **Mo** 6, 203 and 180, **Mo** 7, 271, **Mo** 8, 325, and perhaps **Mo** 6, 212.

Of the five *malmariée* motets that reveal an intertextual nexus with other motets (**Mo** 6, 233, **Mo** 2, 23, **Mo** 5, 142, **Mo** 5, 148, **Mo** 2, 30), the transmission profile of the shared refrains for three of them supports a claim for a connection of Parisian **Mo** with **N(mo)** and also with **W2**. As discussed in Chapter 6, two *malmariée* motets based on *POR-TARE*, **Mo** 6, 233 and **Mo** 5, 148, share refrains with additional motets that appear in **N(mo)** and **W2** at most a folio apart in each manuscript. For **Mo** 6, 233, its sharing of vdB 1691 occurs directly with a motet in those two sources, while **Mo** 5, 148's sharing of vdB 750 with those two sources may have occurred through the intermediary of another motet in fascicle 5, **Mo** 5, 97. Musical evidence does not indicate a clear-cut direction of borrowing between the motets or sources. Nonetheless, the presence of the Artesian **N(mo)** in the transmission profile of refrains shared with other motets within two *malmariée* motets on *POR-TARE* is consequential when considered within the entire *malmariée* corpus.[9] Namely, another *malmariée* motet, **Mo** 2, 30 on *FIAT*, also

---

9 An observation about the chant from which *PORTARE* is derived is in order. In an earlier study, I concluded that *Alleluia. Dulcis virgo* is probably the Marian contrafact of *Alleluia Dulce lignum* (see Chapter 2, note 14 for a citation of this article). The contrafact was probably not Parisian, but used in some northern French locales, possibly in connection with the Assumption or a Marian votive Mass. Specifically, I was able to locate the Marian contrafact in one source connected with Rouen (Paris, BnF lat. 904), and in one source whose other contents suggest connections with Reims and Paris (Biblioteca Comunale di Assisi, 695), but not in other sources

shares its refrain, vdB 1540, with several other motets found in **Mo** and its concordances, including a two-voice motet that appears in **Mo** 6, 231 and **N(mo)**. As was true for the *PORTARE* instances, **Mo** 2, 30 involves intertextuality among motets and includes **N(mo)** in the transmission nexus.[10] Of the three relevant *malmariée* motets, **Mo** 6, 233 offers the greatest likelihood of direct connection to **N(mo)** because it has a concordance in that manuscript.

A further reflection on the Assumption tenor *PORTARE* and its motet interactions is in order: this relatively small corpus gives it a prominent presence in three motets (**Mo** 6, 233, **Mo** 5, 148, **Mo** 5, 142). **Mo** 5, 148 creates its intertextual nexus with other motets on diverse tenors in **Mo**'s fascicle 5. On the other hand, **Mo** 6, 233 shares its refrain with a motet transmitted in **W2** and **N(mo)**, based on another Assumption tenor, *Alleluia. Hodie Maria virgo*; in this second motet, one can reasonably interpret the refrain's female speaker as a married woman who, like the one in **Mo** 6, 233, parodies the selfless Mary, devoted Bride of Christ, evoked in its Assumption tenor. The two shared refrains of **Mo** 5, 142 appear in the unequivocal *malmariée* motet, **Mo** 2, 23, based on the Ascension tenor ET GAUDEBIT, whose *malmariée* parodies the offer of comfort and assurance of steadfastness expressed in the motetus and tenor. Accordingly, allowing for the smallness of the corpus, one cautiously notes that the parodic treatment of the *malmariée* in motets seems to have given rise to additional examples, particularly in connection with the feast of the Assumption.

In sum, the total source profile of the *malmariée* motets suggests that this repertory appeared in a limited number of motet manuscripts: **Mo** (produced in Paris), **W2** (probably produced in Paris), and

---

associated with Rouen or Reims, nor in another twenty-one northern French chant sources. The question of the origins of the Marian contrafact invites more scrutiny. Pesce, "Beyond Glossing," in *Hearing the Motet*, 39–40.

10 **Mo** 2, 30's motetus includes a reference to "the wisest lady in all of Angers." Though this mention of a city in western France does not automatically signal for the motet an origin or provenance in Angers, it is still noteworthy.

Of the five motets in this subgroup, all but **Mo** 6, 233 (i.e. **Mo** 2, 23; **Mo** 5, 142; **Mo** 5, 148; **Mo** 2, 30) also share their refrains with other genres, though intertextuality with motets seems to feature more prominently in their composition. **Mo** 5, 148's refrain 1 also occurs in a song whose sources are linked to Picardy-Artois, and no. 4 appears in two songs whose sources are connected to Picardy-Artois, Artois, or specifically Arras. Refrain no. 4 is also found in *Court de Paradis*, one of whose sources is from northern France. **Mo** 5, 142 and **Mo** 2, 23 share vdB 900 with a *chanson avec des refrains* about whose composer nothing is known, but whose sources are associated with Picardy-Artois. **Mo** 2, 30 shares its refrains with *L'Art d'amours*, whose provenance is unknown.

several manuscripts from northern France—**R(mo)** and **N(mo)** of Artesian origin and **Douce 308** from Lorraine. The earliest source among these is **W2**, mid-thirteenth century, which preserves **Mo** 6, 203. The next MS in terms of dating is MS **R(mo)**, copied after 1253, probably 1260s or 1270s in Artois, possibly in Arras, which contains EM 310. **Mo** 6, 180 may also be early, given that a clausula version survives in **F**, no. 452, fol. 184r, and current scholarly opinion is that the clausula is a transcribed motet. If this speculation is correct, then this motet could date from as early as the 1240s, transmitted in a source that no longer exists. Accordingly, **Mo** 6, 203, EM 310, and **Mo** 6, 180 are likely the earliest motets in this corpus.

Outside of these three early cases, eleven motets fall within the old corpus of **Mo** (late 1270s and 1280s): two in fascicle 2 (23 and 30), four in fascicle 5 (142, 148, 156, 169), three in fascicle 6 (212, 233, 243), and two in fascicle 7 (271 and 276). The four remaining examples are later: **Mo** 8, 325 is the only *malmariée* motet in fascicle 8, probably compiled at the juncture of the thirteenth and fourteenth centuries. **Douce 308**, dated to the early fourteenth century, transmits EM 389 and 415, and **Tu**, dated to ca. 1300, transmits a unicum double motet on f. 16.

As for *malmariée* motet concordances, **N(mo)** was probably copied ca. 1270s, as was **ArsB**, which contains the unusual tenor shared with **Mo** 6, 212. **Mo** 6, 243 has a clausula concordance in the Parisian **StV**, dated to 1270–1300, probably a reworking of the **Mo** motet, and a three-voice version in **Tu**, ca. 1300. Other concordant manuscripts, mostly preserving a single example, fall near to **Mo**'s dating, postdate **Mo**, or are equivocally dated.

Based on this information, yet recognizing the relatively small size of the corpus, one can cautiously speak of a time in which the *malmariée* motet was cultivated: eleven examples within **Mo**'s old corpus suggest the 1270s–1280s. These motets indicate an interest in building upon the topos: **Mo** 2, 23 and **Mo** 5, 142 share two refrains and reveal similar intergeneric play, suggesting one is modeled on the other. **Mo** 5, 148 and **Mo** 2, 30 each individually use refrains that appear in other motets in **Mo** to serve their *malmariée* constructions. **Mo** 6, 233 shares its refrain with another motet based on an Assumption tenor, though in this case the evidence for building upon the topos is not found in **Mo**, but in the roughly contemporaneous **N(mo)**, where the two motets appear one folio apart. Two *malmariée* motets in **Mo**, fascicle 5 are based on the Assumption tenor VERITATEM: **Mo** 5, 156 is a unicum, while **Mo** 5, 169 has a double Latin motet concordance in **Mo** 4, 64. These two *malmariée* motets on the tenor VERITATEM occur in relatively close proximity within fascicle 5 of **Mo**, just as do two motets on

124 *Conclusion*

PORTARE (**Mo** 5, 142 and 5, 148), suggesting a deliberate compilation plan. Four examples in the old corpus of **Mo** (6, 212; 6, 243; 7, 271; 7, 276) do not connect to other *malmariée* motets in the way the seven just described do. Nonetheless, their apparently newly composed status in the old corpus of **Mo**, with no surviving concordances of an earlier dating, is suggestive of a tendency to favor this topos in the 1270s and 1280s. The tendency is also supported by the inclusion in the old corpus of two apparently earlier *malmariée* motets: **Mo** 6, 203 linked to **W2**, and **Mo** 6, 180 to **F**.

Combining this information on dating with the issues of transmission and cultivation, the Parisian **Mo** (late 1270s or 1280s), with its fourteen of eighteen surviving *malmarieée* motets, occupies a central role. The Artesian manuscript **N(mo)**, roughly contemporaneous with **Mo**, participates in the profile of five *malmariée* motets: a source of EM 310, concordance of **Mo** 6, 233, and transmitter of other motets that share refrains with three *malmariée* motets in **Mo**. Particularly striking is **N(mo)**'s concordance for **Mo** 6, 233 (**N(mo)**, fol. 194v, no. 80), because it appears adjacent to another Assumption motet on fol. 195r–v (no. 84), whose female speaker *might* be a *malmariée*. **N(mo)** presents a third treatment of the *malmariée* topos relatively nearby on fol. 191v (EM 310). Given **N(mo)**'s connection to Arras, where the Virgin, particularly her Assumption, was celebrated, this concentrated treatment of the *malmariée*, who stands in a parodic relationship to the Virgin, is noteworthy.

In summary, this study has explored one particular topos, the *malmariée*, within the thirteenth-century motet. Though only eighteen examples survive, they present a rich view of how the concept of the unhappily married woman was treated in this polyphonic genre. The motets set up a play between a *malmariée* text and the message of the liturgical chant that undergirds the polyphony, and also with other genres known from the chanson tradition, in particular the *grand chanson courtois* and the *pastourelle*. These various levels of interaction invite different layers of interpretation on the part of listeners, depending on their knowledge of Church dogma on marriage, of liturgical chant, and of secular song and literature. An individual might hear allegory and/or parody, acceptance or criticism of the norms associated with marriage, and of the treatment of women in general. Some of the motets incorporate all of these possibilities in tour-de-force constructions.

The manuscript evidence suggests a lively interest in the *malmariée* topos in the 1270s and 1280s, witnessed by the compilation of eleven apparently new examples in the old corpus of Montpellier, as well as of two that predate **Mo**. The contemporaneous Artesian manuscript **N(mo)** plays some role in the cultivation and transmission of the topos, but with fewer numbers, as is also the case with the earlier **W2**, probably produced in Paris. The evidence of this study supports other scholars' claims that these three manuscripts intersected in some way. Significantly, for several of the new *malmariée* motets, the creators mined other motets within **Mo** as a source of their refrains. **Mo** 2, 23 and **Mo** 5, 142 even share two refrains and a schema of internal intergeneric play, with the fascicle 5 motet probably a creative response to the fascicle 2 motet. The same impulse seems to have resulted in the adjacent Assumption motets in **N(mo)** at roughly the same time. This study of the *malmariée* in the thirteenth-century motet thus illuminates how the genre's creators fashioned new motets not only through intertextuality with other genres, but also within the motet repertory itself. Through these various sorts of intertexuality, they positioned the *malmariée* within a more nuanced and multifaceted view of gender issues in thirteenth-century society.

Appendix A
Tables 1–7

128 Appendix A

Table 1 Summary of malmariée motet corpus

EM no.	Mo no.	No. of voices, upper-voice text incipit and Gennrich no.	Tenor incipit, Ludwig M(ass) or O(ffice) no., chant source and its liturgical association	Motet concordances	Links to other motets through refrains	Possible interpretation(s)	Manner of presentation
	Mo 6, 180 (f. 232v)	2-voice French *A tort sui d'amours blasmée* 241	[IMMO]LATUS M14 *Alleluia. Pascha nostrum* – EASTER	**F**, no. 452, f. 184r (2-voice clausula)		Parody (and allegory)	Monologue by a woman. *Chanson pieuse* with refrain from a *chanson de malmariée* that says she is criticized for loving
EM 178	Mo 6, 203 (f. 224r)	2-voice French *Hier matin jouer m'en alai* 238	[IMMO]LATUS M14 *Alleluia. Pascha nostrum* – EASTER	**W2**, f. 234r		Parody	Encounter frame (*parmi une pree chevauchai*); overhears dialogue between husband and wife
	Mo 6, 212 (f. 249r)	2-voice French *Amis, vostre demorée* 829a	DECANTATUR Responsory *Ante dies exitus* – GAUDEAT HUNGARIA OFFICE FOR ST. ELIZABETH	Unicum		Allegory or parody	Monologue by a woman to a lover, with mention of beatings by the jealous one

EM 322	2-voice French *Hier matin me chevauchoie* 273	**Mo 6**, 233 (f. 260r)	**N(mo)**, f. 194v (no. 80)	PORTARE M22 *Alleluia. Dulcis virgo* – OCTAVE OF ASSUMPTION/ *Alleluia. Dulce lignum* – INVENTION AND EXALTATION OF THE CROSS	Parody	Encounter frame (*chevauchoie dejouste un vergier flori*); overhears a woman's monologue complaining about her husband
			vdB 1691 ALLELUIA. HODIE MARIA VIRGO M34 **W2**, ff. 227v–228r; **N(mo)**, f. 195r–v (no. 84)			
EM 310	2-voice French *Pour quoi m'avez vous done* 353	**Mo 6**, 243 (f. 265v)	**StV**, f. 288v (2-voice clausula with motetus text incipit); 3-voice **Tu**, ff. 27–28	DOCEBIT M26 *Alleluia. Paraclitus spiritus sanctus* – VESPERS ON THURSDAY AT PENTECOST	Allegory (or secular reading of the tenor)	Monologue by wife to her mother complaining about her arranged marriage
	2-voice French *Ja ne mi marierai* 367		**R(mo)**, f. 209v; **N(mo)**, f. 191v (no. 63)	AMORIS M27 *Alleluia. Veni sancte spiritus* – PENTECOST	Allegory or parody	Monologue by a woman against marriage
EM 389	Single French text *Ostés lou moi* 1100		**Douce 308**, f. 244v (257v)			Monologue by wife complaining about her husband
EM 415	Single French text *Trop sui jonette maris* 1124		**Douce 308**, f. 246v (259v)			Monologue by wife to her husband

(*Continued*)

130 Appendix A

EM no.	Mo no.	No. of voices, upper-voice text incipit and Gennrich no.	Tenor incipit, Ludwig M(ass) or O(ffice) no., chant source and its liturgical association	Motet concordances	Links to other motets through refrains	Possible interpretations(s)	Manner of presentation
EM 273	Mo 2, 23 (f. 29v)	4-voice French *Dame cui j'aim et desir* 334; *Amours vaint tout fors cuer felon* 335; *Au tens d'esté que cil oisel* 336	ET GAUDEBIT M24 *Alleluia. Nos vos relinquam* – ASCENSION	3-voice **Ba** no. 10 (f. 5v), **LoV**, f. 164v; text incipit **Bes** no. 47	**vdB 587** PORTARE M22 **Mo** 5, 142, f. 194r **vdB 900** PORTARE M22 **Mo** 5, 142, f. 193r **vdB 664** NOSTRUM M14 **Mo** 5, 106 (f. 147v) **vdB 664** [AGMINA] M65 **Mo** 5, 108 (f. 148v)	Parody (and allegory)	Triplum opens with unidentified first-person encomium to Love's power, which includes making a lady love another and deceive her husband; then quotes a woman's 6 sung refrains (she addresses her husband in 1 of these, mentions her lover in 5, and compares husband to lover in 3)
	Mo 5, 142 (f. 192v)	3-voice French *Nus ne set les biens d'amors* 286; *Ja Dieus ne me doinst corage* 287	PORTARE M22 *Alleluia. Dulcis virgo* – OCTAVE OF ASSUMPTION/ *Alleluia. Dulce lignum* – INVENTION AND EXALTATION OF THE CROSS	Unicum	**vdB 587** ET GAUDEBIT M24 **Mo** 2, 23, f. 33vb **vdB 900** ET GAUDEBIT M24 **Mo** 2, 23, f. 34vb	Parody	Motetus monologue by wife comparing husband to lover, with closing address to husband

Appendix A   131

Mo 5, 148 (f. 199v)	3-voice French *Si com aloie jouer* 288; *Deduisant com fins amourous* 289	PORTARE M22 *Alleluia. Dulcis virgo* – OCTAVE OF ASSUMPTION/ *Alleluia. Dulce lignum* – INVENTION AND EXALTATION OF THE CROSS	Text incipit **Bes** no. 39	**vdB 532** OMNES M1 Mo 5, 80 (f. 118v); **Ba** no. 90 (f. 56v) **vdB 532** ET SUPER M66 Mo 5, 101 (f. 141v) **vdB 750** ET SUPER M66 Mo 5, 97 (f. 137v); **W2**, f. 228v; **N(mo)**, f. 194v (no. 79); clausula **StV**, f. 291r IN SECULUM M13 Mo 5, 162 (f. 212v) **vdB 1781** OMNES M1 Mo 5, 115 (f. 157v); **Ba** no. 91 (f. 57r)	Parody	Encounter frame in triplum and duplum (*Si com aloie jouer*/ *Deduisant com fins amourous*); overhears women complaining about husbands and wanting to thwart them; triplum mentions lover twice
Mo 5, 156 (f. 207v)	3-voice French *Je sui jonete et jolie* 465; *Hé! Dieus, je n'ai pas mari* 466	VERITATEM M37 Gradual *Propter veritatem. Audi filia* – ASSUMPTION	Unicum			Triplum and motetus monologue by wife who complains about husband and refers to present lover or taking one
Mo 5, 169 (f. 218v)	3-voice French *Li jalous par tout son fustat* 467; *Tuit cil qui sunt enamourat* 468	VERITATEM M37 Gradual *Propter veritatem. Audi filia* – ASSUMPTION	Double Latin **Mo** 4, 64 (f. 102v)			Third-person invitation to those in love to dance; the queen wants them to thrash the jealous who wear a horn on their foreheads and drive them from the dance

(*Continued*)

132 Appendix A

EM no.	Mo no.	No. of voices, upper-voice text incipit and Gennrich no.	Tenor incipit, Ludwig M(ass) or O(ffice) no.. chant source and its liturgical association	Motet concordances	Links to other motets through refrains	Possible interpretations(s)	Manner of presentation
	Mo 7, 271 (f. 300v)	3-voice French *Dame bele et avenant et de biau port* 872; *Fi, mari, de vostre amour!* 873	French tenor: NUS N'IERT JA JOLIS, S'IL N'AIME	Unicum			Motetus monologue by wife who mentions husband and lover
	Mo 7, 276 (f. 308v)	3-voice French [*Nus ne se doit...*] 601a (922); [*Je sui en melencolie...*] 601b (923)	AVE VERUM CORPUS M84 Eucharistic chant	*Ave verum* as upper-voice text **Hu** ff. 124v (12c) & 122v (935i)			Motetus monologue by an unhappily married husband
	Mo 8, 325 (f. 375v)	3-voice French *S'on me regarde, s'on me regarde* 908; *Prennés i garde, s'on me regarde* 909	French tenor: HE MI ENFANT	Unicum			Paired triplum and motetus: monologue by woman who is attracted to one man and wants to thwart another who is "jealous of me" (*jalous de moi*)

EM 213	**Mo** 2, 30 (f. 45v)	4-voice French *Cest quadruple sans raison* 798; *Vous n'i dormirés jamais* 799; *Biaus cuers renvoisies et douz* 800	FIAT O54 Responsory *Benedictus dominus. Replebitur majestate eius omnia terra fiat fiat* – HOLY TRINITY SATURDAY VESPERS	**Cl** no 8 (f. 371v); double Latin **Ba** no. 3 (f. 2v)	Unlikely intended as parody or allegory	Triplum monologue by woman who rejects a man whom she calls *vilains*, but it is unclear whether he is her husband or a suitor
				vdB 1540 EIUS O16 4-voice **Mo** 2, 22 (f. 27v), **Cl** no. 51 (f. 389r); 3-voice **Mo** 5, 145 (f. 195v), **Ba** no. 41 (f. 23r) **vdB 1540** FLOS FILIUS E[IUS] O16 2-voice **Mo** 6, 231 (f. 259), **N(mo)**, f. 180v (no. 9)		
Other		3-voice French *Biaus dous amis, quel conseil me donrés?* 776a; *Grant pechiet fist cis qui m'a mariée* 776b	VALE O49 Marian antiphon *Ave regina caelorum*	**Tu**, f. 16 unicum	Parody	Triplum and motetus monologues by wife, addressed to her lover. In triplum, she asks her lover's advice in handling her husband; in motetus, she laments that the time she spends with her lover is short

Appendix A 133

134 *Appendix A*

Table 2 Seven motets that share refrains with other genres

Refrain no. (vdB)

1006	1374	1463	1822	189	1856	1555	1531
Ja ne mi marierai	*Ne vos mariez mie*	*Ostez moi, l'anelet du doit*	*Tuit cil qui sunt enamourat*	*A tort sui d'amors blasmeie*	*Vous diroiz ce que vous voudroiz*	*Quant pluz me bat*	*Prendés i garde*

MOTET SOURCE

1006	1374	1463	1822	189	1856	1555	1531
			Mo 5, 169, f. 219r (2x) (M) **Mo** 4, 64, f. 103r (2x) (M) Latin version	**Mo** 6, 180, f. 232v (M)	**Mo** 6, 203, f. 249r (M) **W2**, f. 234r (M)	**Mo** 6, 212, f. 249r (M)	**Mo** 8, 325, f. 375 (373)va/vb (2x) (M1)
R(mo), f. 209vb (M), EM 310 **N(mo)**, f. 191v (M), EM 310	**R(mo)**, f. 209vb (M), EM 310 **N(mo)**, f. 191v (M), EM 310	**Douce 308** f. 244 (257)va, EM 389					

CHANSON SOURCE (trouvère, unless otherwise noted)

1006	1374	1463	1822	189	1856	1555	1531
C, f. 44v, chanson avec des refrains (Jacquemin de la Vente)				**C**, f. 117r, chanson avec des refrains			

K, p. 158b, chanson avec des refrains (Perrin d'Angicourt)	K, p. 338a (M), pastourelle avec des refrains	
N(trv), f. 50vb, chanson avec des refrains (Perrin d'Angicourt)	N(trv), f. 163rv (M) pastourelle avec des refrains	
P, f. 131vb, chanson avec des refrains (Perrin d'Angicourt)	P, f. 186vb (M), pastourelle avec des refrains	M, f. 108vb (M), chanson avec des refrains 2 (Guillaume le Vinier)
	T, f. 171v (M), pastourelle avec des refrains	T, f. 29r, chanson avec des refrains 2 (Guillaume le Vinier)
	U, ff. 154r & 157r, pastourelle avec des refrains	U, f. 72v, chanson avec des refrains
V, f. 72ra, chanson avec des refrains		U, f. 55v, chanson avec des refrains 1
X, f. 108ra, chanson avec des refrains (Perrin d'Angicourt)	X, f. 221vb (M), pastourelle avec des refrains	M, f. 188vb (M), chanson à refrain (Moniot d'Arras)
		T, f. 118r, chanson à refrain (Moniot d'Arras)

Appendix A 135

(*Continued*)

Appendix A

Refrain no. (vdB)

1006	1374	1463	1822	189	1856	1555	1531	
Ja ne mi marierai	Ne vos mariez mie	Ostez moi, l'anelet du doit	Tuit cil qui sunt enamourat	A tort sui d'amors blasmeie	Vous diroiz ce que vous voudroiz	Quant pluz me bat	Prendés i garde	
							a. f. 44(48)rb, chanson à refrain (Moniot d'Arras)	**a.** f. 119 (136)va, (M1), rondeau (Guillaume d'Amiens)
				R(trb), f. 29ra, chanson avec des refrains (Thibaut de Blaison)				
				Mod. R.4.4, f. 229ra, chanson avec des refrains	**Mod. R.4.4**, f. 217vb, chanson avec des refrains 1			
					Z, f. 32v, chanson avec des refrains 2			

OTHER

Violette	Court d'amours II	La Court de Paradis				Quinque		Renart
Pa 1374, f. 133vb	**Pa 1731**, f. 61va	**Pa 837**, f. 59rb				**Vat. 71**, f. 50 (XVII)v		**Pa 1593**, f. 48 (49)vb (M2)
Pa 1553, f. 286v		**Pa 25532**, f. 334ra (M)				**Tr 1890**, f. 206vb		**Pa 25566**, f. 165rb (M1)
SP 4° v. XIV 3, f. 3ra		**Pa 1802**, f. 102r				**KBR 2475–81**, f. 79r		**Pa 372**, f. 50va (M1)
NY M. 36, f. 4								**Pa 1581**, f. 48ra

(M) indicates a refrain is transmitted with music notation; different melodies are distinguished as M1, M2, and so on.

Appendix A   137

Table 3 **Mo** 7, 271 refrain transmission.

Refrain number (*VdB*)	746 *Fi, maris, de vostre amour*	1407 *Nus n'iert ja joli*	1842 *Vilains, vous demorrés*
MOTET SOURCE	**Mo** 7, 271, f. 300vb (M1) **Vat. 1543**, no. 5	**Mo** 7, 271, f. 301ra (2x) (M) **Vat. 1543**, no. 5 (2x) (M)	**Mo** 7, 271, f. 301rb (M) **Vat. 1543**, no. 5 (M)
CHANSON SOURCE (trouvère, unless otherwise noted)	**W**, f. 33rb (M1), polyphonic rondeau (Adam de la Halle)	**k**, f. 79v, rondeau	
OTHER	*Renart* **Pa 1593**, f. 50 (51)vb (M2) **Pa 25566**, f. 167va (M1)	*Court d'amours II* **Pa 1731**, f. 60va	

(M) indicates a refrain is transmitted with music notation; differing melodies are distinguished as M1, M2, and so on

Table 4 **Mo** 6, 233 refrain transmission.

Refrain no. (*vdB*)	1691 *Se j'osoie*
MOTET SOURCE	**Mo** 6, 233, f. 260r, motet 1 (M) **W2**, f. 228r, motet 2 (M) **N(mo)**, f. 194v, motet 1 (M) **N(mo)**, f. 195v, motet 2 (M)

(**M**) indicates a refrain is transmitted with music notation; differing melodies are distinguished as **M1**, **M2**, and so on.

Table 5 **Mo** 5, 148 refrain transmission.

Refrain no. (vdb)	532 Dex, je n'i os aler	750 Fines amouretes ai trouvées	1489 Pleüst a Dieu	1781 Toz li cuers me rit de joie
MOTET SOURCE				
	Motet 1: **Mo** 5, 148, f. 199v (M)	Motet 1: **Mo** 5, 148, f. 199v (M1)	**Mo** 5, 148, ff. 200v & 201r (M)	Motet 1: **Mo** 5, 148, f. 200v (M)
	Motet 2: **Mo** 5, 80, f. 120r (M)	Motet 2: **Mo** 5, 97, f. 139r (M1)		Motet 2: **Mo** 5, 115, f. 158r (M)
	Motet 3: **Mo** 5, 101, f. 141v (M)	Motet 3: **Mo** 5, 162, f. 213v (M2) motet 2: **W2**, f. 228v (M1), 2-voice		
	Motet 2: **Ba** no. 90 f. 56vb (M)			Motet 2: **Ba** no. 91, f. 57rb (M)
	Motet 1: **Bes**, no. 39	Motet 1: **Bes**, no. 39 Motet 2: **N(mo)**, f. 194v (M1) Motet 2: **Stv**, f. 291r (M1), related 2-voice clausula	**Bes**, no. 39	Motet 1: **Bes**, no. 39

CHANSON SOURCE (trouvère, unless otherwise noted)

K, p. 353b, chanson avec des refrains (Pierrot de Douai)			**K**, p. 207a, chanson avec des refrains 1 (Jean Erart) **M**, f. 129rb, chanson avec des refrains 2 (Colard li Bouteiller)

Appendix A 139

N(trv), f. 171vb, chanson avec des refrains (Perrot de Douai)

X, f. 230rb, chanson avec des refrains (Perrot de Douai)

M, fol. 177ra, chanson avec des refrains 1 (Guiot de Dijon)
N(trv), f. 99vb, chanson avec des refrains 1 (Jean Erart)

P, f. 95b, chanson avec des refrains 1 (Jean Erart)
T, f. 136v, chanson avec des refrains 1 (Adrieu Contredit)
X, f. 144r a, chanson avec des refrains 2 (Jean Erart)

a, f. 74 (72)va, chanson avec des refrains 2 (Colard le Bouteiller)

OTHER

L'art d'amours
Pa 881, f. 82ra,
Pa 2741, f. 42ra
Mod. g.G.3.20, f. 48r
KBR 10988, f. 66v
La Court de Paradis
Pa 837, f. 59va
Pa 25532, f. 334va (M)
Pa 1802, f. 104r
Roman de Fauvel
Pa 146, f. 24va (M)

(M) indicates a refrain is transmitted with music notation; differing melodies are distinguished as M1, M2, and so on

Table 6 **Mo** 2, 23 and **Mo** 5, 142 refrain transmission.

Refrain no. (vdb)	587 Doleroz mari	286 Bon jour et hennor	900 Ja Dex ne mi doint corage	971 J'ai plus chier un dous baisier	664 E[n] non Diu, amors me tienent	748 Fines amouretes ai et bel ami joli
MOTET SOURCE						
	Motet 1: **Mo** 2, 23, f. 33vb (M) Motet 2: **Mo** 5,142, f. 194r (M)	**Mo** 2, 23, f. 33vb (M)	Motet 1: **Mo** 2, 23, f. 34vb (M) Motet 2: **Mo** 5, 142, f. 193r (M)	**Mo** 2, 23, f. 34vb (M)	Motet 1: **Mo** 2, 23, f. 35vb (M1) Motet 2: **Mo** 5, 106, f. 147v (M1) Motet 3: **Mo** 5, 108, f. 150v (M2)	**Mo** 2, 23, f. 35vb (M)
	Motet 1: **Ba** no. 10, f. 6ra (M)	**Ba** no. 10, f. 6ra (M)	Motet 1: **Ba** no. 10, f. 6va (M)	**Ba** no. 10, f. 6va (M)	Motet 1: **Ba** no. 10, f. 6va (M1)	**Ba** no. 10, f. 6va (M)
	Motet 1: **LoV**, f. 164v (M)	**LoV**, f. 164v (M)	Motet 1: **LoV**, f. 164v (M)	**LoV**, f. 164v (M)	Motet 1: **LoV**, f. 164v (M1)	**LoV**, f. 164v (M)
	Motet 1: **Bes**, no. 47	**Bes**, no. 47	Motet 1: **Bes**, no. 47	**Bes**, no. 47	Motet 1: **Bes**, no. 47 Motet 4: **Douce 308**, f. 246 (259)rb	**Bes**, no. 47

Appendix A 141

CHANSON SOURCE (trouvère, unless otherwise noted)

K, p. 257b, chanson avec des refrains (Philippe Paon)
N (trv), f. 126rb, chanson avec des refrains (Philippe Paon)
P, f. 115ra, chanson avec des refrains (Jeannot Paon)
R (trv), f. 93v, chanson avec des refrains
X, f. 173vε, chanson avec des refrains (Philippe Paon)

(M) indicates a refrain is transmitted with music notation; differing melodies are distinguished as M1, M2, and so on

142 *Appendix A*

Table 7 **Mo** 2, 30 refrain transmission.

Refrain no. (vdb)	1867 *Voz n'i dormirés jamais*	217 *Biaus cuers renvoisiés et douz*	1540 *Puis que bele dame m'aime*
MOTET SOURCE			
	Mo 2, 30, f. 45vb (M)	**Mo** 2, 30, f. 46ra (M)	Motet 1: **Mo** 2, 30, f. 46va (M), 4-voice
			Motet 2: **Mo** 2, 22, f. 29va (M), 4-voice
			Motet 2: **Mo** 5, 145, f. 196v (M), 3-voice
			Motet 3: **Mo** 6, 231, f. 259r (M), 2-voice
			Motet 2: **Ba** no. 41, f. 23r (M), 3-voice
	Cl no. 8, f. 371va (M)	**Cl** no. 8, f. 371vb	Motet 1, **Cl** no. 8, f. 371va (M), 4-voice
			Motet 2: **Cl** no. 51, f. 389v (M), 4-voice
			Motet 3: **N(mo)**, f. 180v (M), 2-voice
OTHER			
	L'art d'amours		*L'art d'amours*
	Pa 881, f. 95rb		**Pa 881**, f. 89vb
	Pa 2741, f. 59va		**Pa 2741**, f. 52va
	Mod. g.G.3.20, f. 70r		**Mod. g.G.3.20**, f. 61v
	KBR 10988, f. 92v		**KBR 10988**, f. 81v

(M) indicates a refrain is transmitted with music notation; differing melodies are distinguished as M1, M2, and so on

Appendix B
Texts and Translations of Motets 60, 62, 67, and 84 from MS N(mo)

The texts and translations derive from *Motets from the Chansonnier de Noailles*, ed. by Gaël Saint-Cricq, with Eglal Doss-Quinby and Samuel N. Rosenberg. *Recent Researches in the Music of the Middle Ages and Early Renaissance*, vol. 42. Middleton, WI: A-R Editions, Inc., 2017. Used with permission. www.areditions.com

No. 60

Mieus voil sentir les maus d'amer *I'd rather feel the woes of love*
ke faillier a amie. *than fail my beloved.*
Tenor *ALLELUIA*

No. 62

Renvoisïement i vois a mon ami. *Merrily I go to my beloved.*
Ensi doit on aler a son ami. *So must one go to one's beloved.*
Tenor *HODIE*

No. 67

J'ai fait ami a mon cois, I have found a sweetheart to my liking,
preu et saige et cortois. worthy and wise and refined.
Si me tieg pour amie, He considers me his sweetheart,
s'alongera ma vie. so my life will be prolonged.
Tenor *GAUDETE*

No. 84

Cele m'a s'amour dounee	She has granted me her love,	vdB 314
ki mon cuer et mon cors a.	the one who's won my heart and body.	
Mieus vient k'amours m'ochient	I'd rather die from love	vdB1334A
k'autres maus autresi me norrie.	than live with any other woe.	
Je vous ai tout mon cuer douné,	I have entrusted my heart to you,	vdB1155
belle tres douce amie.	dearest sweet beloved.	
Je ne l'ai mie	My heart belongs	vdB1084
Avoc moi mon cuer,	not to me,	
ains l'a m'amie.	but to my beloved.	
É Dieus! É Dieus! verrai je ja le jour	Oh God! Oh God! Will I ever see the day	vdB 835
ke l'aie ens ma baillie?	when I have her in my sway?	
Ce m'ochist quant je ne vous voi	It kills me when I don't see you	vdB 321
plus sovent,	more often,	
douce amie.	sweet love.	
Cuers dous, ne m'obliés mie,	Tender heart, don't forget me,	vdB 383
se je ne vous voi sovent.	even if I don't see you often.	
Dieus! li cuers me faura ja,	God! My heart will soon fail me,	vdB 539
tant la desir vëoir!	so eagerly do I yearn to see her!	
Nus ne set mes maus	No one knows my pains	vdB 1402
s'il n'aime	who is not in love	
ou s'il n'a amé.	Or has not been.	
J'aim belle damoiselle,	I'm in love with a beautiful maiden,	vdB 941
mal ait ki mi nuira!	damn anyone who'd do me harm!	
Je les senc,	I feel them,	vdB 1059
les tres dous maus d'amer!	the very sweet pains of love!	
Se j'osoie,	If I dared,	vdB 1691
Je feroie ami.	I'd take a lover.	

Tenor *ALLELUIA. HODIE MARIA VIRGO CELOS ASCENDIT. GAUDETE, QUIA CUM CHRISTO REGNAT*

Bibliography

Altmann, Barbara K., and Carleton W. Carroll, eds. *The Court Reconvenes: Courtly Literature across the Disciplines.* Cambridge: D. S. Brewer, 2003.
Atchison, Mary. *The Chansonnier of Oxford Bodleian MS Douce 308: Essays and Complete Edition of Texts.* Aldershot and Burlington, VT: Ashgate, 2005.
Aubry, Elizabeth. "The Dialectic between Occitania and France in the Thirteenth Century." *Early Music History* 16 (1997): 1–53.
———. *The Music of the Troubadours.* Bloomington: Indiana University Press, 1996.
Baldwin, John W. "Consent and the Marital Debt: Five Discourses in Northern France around 1200." In *Consent and Coercion to Sex and Marriage in Ancient and Medieval Societies*, edited by Angeliki E. Laiou, 257–70. Washington, DC: Dumbarton Oaks, 1993.
———. *The Language of Sex. Five Voices from Northern France around 1200.* Chicago and London: University of Chicago Press, 1994.
Baltzer, Rebecca. "The Decoration of Montpellier 8: Its Place in the Continuum of Parisian Manuscript Illumination." In *The Montpellier Codex: The Final Fascicle*, edited by Catherine A. Bradley and Karen Desmond, 78–89. Woodbridge and Rochester, NY: Boydell Press, 2018.
———. "The Polyphonic Progeny of an *Et gaudebit*: Assessing Family Relations in the Thirteenth-Century Motet." In *Hearing the Motet: Essays on the Motet of the Middle Ages and Renaissance*, edited by Dolores Pesce, 18–27. New York and Oxford: Oxford University Press, 1997.
Bec, Pierre. *La Lyrique française au Moyen Âge: XIIe–XIIIe siècles. Contribution à une typologie des genres poétiques médiévaux.* 2 vols. Paris: Picard, 1977–78.
———. "Quelques réflexions sur la poésie lyrique médiéval: Problèmes et essai de caractérisation." In *Mélanges offerts à Rita Lejeune*, 2 vols. 2: 1309–29. Gembloux: Duculot, 1969.
———. "'Trobairitz' et chansons de femme: Contribution à la connaissance du lyrisme féminin au moyen âge." *Cahiers de civilisation médiévale* 22 (1979): 235–62.

Bleisch, Nicholas W. "The Copying and Collection of Music in the Trouvère Chansonnier F-Pn fr. 24406." Ph.D. diss.: King's College, University of Cambridge, 2018.

Blonquist, Lawrence B, trans. *L'Art d'amours* (The Art of Love). Garland Library of Medieval Literature, series A, vol. 32. New York and London: Garland Publishing, Inc., 1987.

Bradley, Catherine A. *Authorship and Identity in Late Thirteenth-Century Motets.* Royal Musical Association Monographs No. 39. Routledge: London and New York, 2022.

———. "Choosing a Thirteenth-Century Motet Tenor: From the *Magnus liber organi* to Adam de la Halle." *JAMS* 72 (2019): 431–92.

———. "Contrafacta and Transcribed Motets: Vernacular Influences on Latin Motets and Clausulae in the Florence Manuscript." *Early Music History* 32 (2013): 1–70.

———. *Polyphony in Medieval Paris: The Art of Composing with Plainchant.* Cambridge: Cambridge University Press, 2018.

———. "Song and Quotation in Two-Voice Motets for Saint Elizabeth of Hungary." *Speculum* 92 (2017): 661–91.

———. ed. with Karen Desmond. *The Montpellier Codex: The Final Fascicle.* Woodbridge and Rochester, NY: Boydell Press, 2018.

———.and Gaël Saint-Cricq, with Christopher Callahan. *An Introduction, Facsimile Reproduction, and Critical Edition of Turin, Biblioteca reale, varia 42.* Lucca: LIM Editrice, forthcoming.

Brundage, James A. "Domestic Violence in Classical Canon Law." In *Violence in Medieval Society*, edited by Richard W. Kaeuper, 183–95. Rochester. NY: Boydell Press, 2000.

———. "Implied Consent to Intercourse." In *Consent and Coercion to Sex and Marriage in Ancient and Medieval Societies*, edited by Angeliki E. Laiou, 245–56. Washington, DC: Dumbarton Oaks, 1993.

———. *Law, Sex, and Christian Society in Medieval Europe.* Chicago, IL: University of Chicago Press, 1987.

———. *Medieval Canon Law.* London: Longman, 1995.

Büttner, Fred, *Das Klauselrepertoire der Handschrift Saint-Victor (Paris, BN, lat. 15139): Eine Studie zur mehrstimmigen Komposition im 13. Jahrhundert.* Lecce: Milella, 2011.

———. ed. *Die Klauseln der Handschrift Saint-Victor (Paris, BN, lat. 15139).* Tutzing: Schneider, 1999.

Buffum, Douglas Labaree, ed. *Le Roman de la Violette ou de Gerart de Nevers par Gerbert de Montreuil.* Paris: H. Champion, 1928.

Burr, Kristin L. "Recreating the Body: Euriaut's Tales in *Le Roman de la Violette.*" *Symposium* 56/1 (Spring 2002): 3–16.

Butterfield, Ardis. *Poetry and Music in Medieval France from Jean Renart to Guillaume de Machaut.* Cambridge: Cambridge University Press, 2002.

Callahan, Christopher. "Collecting Trouvère Lyric at the Peripheries: The Lessons of MSS Paris, BnF fr. 20050 and Bern, Burgerbibliothek 389." *Textual Cultures* 8/2 (Fall 2013): 15–30.

———. "Thibaut de Champagne and Disputed Attributions: The Case of MSS Bern, Burgerbibliothek 389 (C) and Paris, BnF fr. 1591(R)." *Textual Cultures* 5/1 (Spring 2010): 111–32.

Catalunya, David. "Music, Space and Ritual in Medieval Castille, 1221–1350." Ph.D. diss., Universität Würzburg, 2016.

Chanter m'estuet: Songs of the Trouvères. Edited by Samuel N. Rosenberg, music edited by Hans Tischler. Bloomington: Indiana University Press, 1981.

Le Court d'Amours de Mahieu le Poirier et la suite anonyme de la "Court d'Amours". Edited by T. Scully. Waterloo, Ont.: Wilfried Laurier University Press, 1976.

Curran, Sean. "Composing a Codex: The Motets in the 'La Clayette' Manuscript." In *Medieval Music in Practice: Studies in Honor of Richard Crocker*, edited by Judith A. Peraino, 219–53. Middleton, WI: American Institute of Musicology, 2013.

———. "A Palaeographical Analysis of the Verbal Text in Montpellier 8: Problems, Implications, Opportunities." In *The Montpellier Codex: The Final Fascicle*, edited by Catherine A. Bradley and Karen Desmond, 32–65. Woodbridge and Rochester, NY: The Boydell Press, 2018.

———. "Writing, Performance, and Devotion in the Thirteenth-Century Motet: The 'La Clayette' Manuscript." In *Manuscripts and Medieval Song: Inscription, Performance, Context*, edited by Helen Deeming and Elizabeth Eva Leach, 193–220. Cambridge: Cambridge University Press, 2015.

Dähne, Rudolf. *Die Lieder der Maumariée seit dem Mittelalter*. Halle: M. Niemeyer, 1933.

d'Avray, David. "The Gospel of the Marriage Feast of Cana and Marriage Preaching in France." In *The Bible in the Medieval World. Essays in Memory of Beryl Smalley*, edited by Katherine Walsh and Diana Wood, 207–24. Oxford and New York: Basil Blackwell, 1985.

———. *Medieval Marriage: Symbolism and Society*. Oxford and New York: Oxford University Press, 2005.

Dell, Helen. *Desire by Gender and Genre in Trouvère Song*. Gallica 10. Woodbridge, Suffolk and Rochester, NY: D. S. Brewer, 2008.

Dolce, Brianne. "'Soit hom u feme': New Evidence for Women Musicians and the Search for the 'Women Trouvères'." *Revue de Musicologie* 106 (2020): 301–28.

Doss-Quinby, Eglal. *Les Refrains chez les trouvères du XIIe siècle au XIVe*. New York: P. Lang, 1984.

Dronke, Peter. *The Medieval Lyric*. 3rd ed. Woodbridge, Suffolk: D. S. Brewer, 1996.

Duby, Georges. "The Matron and the Mis-Married Woman: Perceptions of Marriage in Northern France circa 1100." In *Social Relations and Ideas: Essays in Honour of R. H. Hilton*, edited by T. H. Aston, P. R. Coss, Christopher Dyer, and Joan Thirsk, 89–108. New York: Cambridge University Press, 1983.

———. *Medieval Marriage: Two Models from Twelfth-Century France*, trans. Elborg Forster. Baltimore, MD and London: The Johns Hopkins University Press, 1978.

148 Bibliography

———. *Women of the Twelfth Century*. Vol. 3: *Eve and the Church*, trans Jean Birrell. Chicago, IL: University of Chicago Press, 1998.

Epstein, Marcia Jenneth, ed. and trans. *'Prions en chantant': Devotional Songs of the Trouvères*. Toronto: University of Toronto Press, 1997.

Evans, Dafydd. "Marie de France, Chrétien de Troyes, and the *Malmariée*." In *Chrétien de Troyes and the Troubadours: Essays in Memory of the Late Leslie Topsfield*, edited by Peter S. Noble and Linda M. Paterson, 159–71. Cambridge: St. Catherine's College, 1984.

Everist, Mark. *French Motets in the Thirteenth Century: Music, Poetry and Genre*. Cambridge: Cambridge University Press, 1994.

———. "Friends and Foals: The Polyphonic Music of Adam de la Halle." In *Musical Culture in the World of Adam de la Halle*, edited by Jennifer Saltzstein, 311–51. Leiden and Boston, MA: Brill, 2019.

———. "Motets, French Tenors, and the Polyphonic Chanson ca. 1300." *The Journal of Musicology* 24 (2007): 365–406.

———. "The Polyphonic 'Rondeau' c. 1300: Repertory and Context." *Early Music History* 15 (1996): 59–96.

———."The Refrain Cento: Myth or Motet?" *Journal of the Royal Music Association* 114 (1989): 164–88.

———. "The Rondeau Motet: Paris and Artois in the Thirteenth Century." *Music & Letters* 69 (1988): 1–22.

Frank, István. "Tuit cil qui sunt enamourat" (Notes de philologie pour l'étude des origines lyriques, II). *Romania* 297 (1954): 98–108.

Gaunt, Simon B. "Marginal Men, Marcabru and Orthodoxy: The Early Troubadours and Adultery." *Medium Ævum* 59 (1990): 55–72.

Gennrich, Friedrich. *Bibliographie des ältestesten französischen und lateinischen Motetten*. Summa musicae Medii Aevi 2. Darmstadt: Friedrich Gennrich, 1957.

Giélée, Jacquemart. *Renart le nouvel, publié d'après le manuscrit La Vallière (B.N. fr. 25566)*, ed. Henri Roussel. Paris: A. & J. Picard, 1961.

Grau, Anna Kathryn. "Representing 'Women's Songs' in Stories: Lyric Interpolations and Female Characters in *Guillaume de Dole* and the *Roman de la Violette*." *Essays in Medieval Studies* 27 (2011): 33–44.

———. "Representation and Resistance: Female Vocality in Thirteenth-Century France." Ph.D diss., University of Pennsylvania, 2010.

Gravdal, Kathryn. *Vilain and Courtois: Transgressive Parody in French Literature of the Twelfth and Thirteenth Centuries*. Lincoln: University of Nebraska Press, 1989.

Grimbert, Joan Tasker. "Songs by Women and Women's Songs: How Useful is the Concept of Register"? In *The Court Reconvenes: Courtly Literature across the Disciplines*, edited by Barbara K. Altmann and Carleton W. Carroll, 117–24. Cambridge: D. S. Brewer, 2003.

Haines, John. *Satire in the Songs of* Renart le nouvel. Geneva: Droz, 2010.

Hoekstra, Gerald R. "The French Motet as Trope: Multiple Levels of Meaning in *Quant florist la violete/El mois de mai/Et gaudebit*." *Speculum* 73 (1998): 32–57.

Huot, Sylvia. *Allegorical Play in the Old French Motet: The Sacred and the Profane in Thirteenth-Century Polyphony*. Stanford, CA: Stanford University Press, 1997.

———. *From Song to Book: The Poetics of Writing in Old French Lyric and Lyrical Narrative Poetry*. Ithaca, NY: Cornell University Press, 1987.

———. "Polyphonic Poetry: The Old French Motet and its Literary Context." *French Forum* 14 (1989): 261–78.

Hurtig, Dolliann Margaret. "'I Do, I DO': Medieval Models of Marriage and Choice of Partners in Marie de France's 'Le Fraisne'." *The Romanic Review* 92: 363–79.

Ibos-Augé, Anne. "La Function des insertions lyriques dans des oeuvres narratives et didactiques aux XIIIe et XIVe siècles." Université de Bordeaux III-Michel de Montaigne 2000.

———. "Récurrences et formules mélodiques dans le roman de *Renart le Nouvel*." Brepols Online, pp. 257–89. https://doi.org/10.1484/M.ARTEM-EB.5.103354.

———. "Refrain Quotations in Adam's Rondeaux, Motets and Plays." In *Musical Culture in the World of Adam de la Halle*, edited by Jennifer Saltzstein, 249–81. Leiden and Boston, MA: Brill, 2019.

———. "Les Refrains de la 'Court de Paradis': Variance et coherence des insertions lyriques dans un poème narrative du XIIIe siècle." *Revue de Musicologie* 93 (2007): 227–67.

Jeanroy, Alfred. *Les Origines de la poésie lyrique en France au moyen âge*. Paris: Hachette, 1889. 4th ed. Paris: Honoré Champion, 1965.

Jenkins, T. Atkinson, ed. *Eructavit: An Old French Metrical Paraphrase of Psalm XLIV Published from All the Known Manuscripts and Attributed to Adam de Perseigne*. Dresden: Die Gesellschaft für romanische Literatur, 1909.

Johnson, Susan M. "The Malmariée Theme in Old French Lyric or What is a *Chanson de Malmariée*?" In *"Chançon legiere a chanter": Essays on Old French Literature in Honor of Samuel N. Rosenberg*, edited by Karen Fresco and Wendy Pfeffer, 133–151. New York: Summa Publications, Inc., 2007.

Karp, Theodore. "Perrin d'Angicourt." In *Grove Music Online*.

Kenney, E. J., ed. *Amores. Medicamina faciei femineae. Ars amatoria. Remedia amoris*. New York: Oxford University Press, 1994.

Klinck, Anne L. "The Oldest Folk Poetry? Medieval Woman's Song as 'Popular' Lyric." In *From Arabye to Engelond: Medieval Studies in Honour of Mahmoud Manzalaoui on His 75th Birthday*, edited by A. E. Christa Canitz and Gernot R. Wieland, 229–52. Ottawa: University of Ottawa Press, 1999.

———. "Singing a Song of Sorrow." In *Laments for the Lost in Medieval Literature*, edited by Jan Tolmie and M. J. Toswell, 1–20. Turnhout: Brepols, 2010.

Larrington, Carolyne. *Women and Writing in Medieval Europe: A Sourcebook*. London and New York: Routledge, 1995.

Leach, Elizabeth Eva, Joseph W. Mason, and Matthew P. Thomson, eds. *A Medieval Songbook: Trouvère MS C.* Woodbridge and Rochester, NY: Boydell Press, 2022.

Leclercq, Jean. "L'Amour et le marriage vus par des clercs et des religieux, spécialement au XIIe siècle." In *Love and Marriage in the Twelfth Century*, edited by Willy Van Hoecke and Andries Welkenhuysen, 102–15. Mediaevalia Lovaniensia ser. 1, studia 8. Leuven: Leuven University Press, 1981.

Linker, Robert White. *A Bibliography of Old French Lyrics.* University, MS: Romance Monographs, Inc., 1979.

Ludwig, Friedrich. *Repertorium organorum recentioris et motetorum vetustissimi stili*, ed. Luther A. Dittmer. 2 vols. in 3. New York: Institute of Mediaeval Music, 1961–78 [1910].

Lug, Robert. "Katharer und Waldenser in Metz: Zur Herkunft der ältesten Sammlung von Trobador-Liedern (1231)." In *Okzitanistik, Altokzitanistik und Provenzalistik: Geschichte und Auftrag einer europäischen Philologie*, edited by Angelica Rieger, 249–74. Frankfurt and Berlin: Lang, 2000.

Makowski, Elizabeth M. "The Conjugal Debt and Canon Law." *Journal of Medieval History* 3 (1977): 99–114.

McDowell, Patricia Anne. "The Malmariée: Intertextuality of the Theme in Twelfth- and Thirteenth-Century French and Occitan Lyric and Narrative Poetry." Ph.D. diss.: University of Washington, 2001.

Ménard, Philippe, ed. *Les Poésies de Guillaume le Vinier.* Geneva: Droz, 1970.

Menuge, Noël James. "Female Wards and Marriage in Romance and Law: A Question of Consent." In *Young Medieval Women*, edited by Katherine J. Lewis et al., 153–71. New York: St. Martin's Press, 1999.

The Montpellier Codex, Part 4: *Texts and Translations.* Translations by Susan Stakel and Joel C. Relihan. Recent Researches in the Music of the Middle Ages and Early Renaissance, vol. 8. Madison, WI: A-R Editions, Inc., 1985.

Motets from the Chansonnier de Noailles. Edited by Gaël Saint-Cricq, with Eglal Doss-Quinby and Samuel N. Rosenberg. Recent Researches in the Music of the Middle Ages and Early Renaissance, vol. 42. Middleton, WI: A-R Editions, Inc., 2017.

Mölk, Ulrich, and Friedrich Woltzettel. *Répertoire métrique de la poésie française des origines à 1350.* Munich: W. Fink Verlag, 1972.

Newman, Barbara. *God and the Goddesses: Vision, Poetry, and Belief in the Middle Ages.* Philadelphia: University of Pennsylvania Press, 2005.

The Old French Ballette: Oxford, Bodleian Library, MS Douce 308. Edited, translated, and introduced by Eglal Doss-Quinby and Samuel N. Rosenberg; music editions and commentary by Elizabeth Aubrey. Geneva: Droz, 2006.

O'Sullivan, Daniel E. "The Northern *Jeu-parti*." In *Musical Culture in the World of Adam de la Halle*, edited by Jennifer Saltzstein, 153–88. Leiden and Boston, MA: Brill, 2019.

Page, Christopher. *The Owl and the Nightingale: Musical Life and Ideas in France 1100–1300.* Berkeley: University of California Press, 1990.

Peraino, Judith A. "Taking *Notae* on King and Cleric: Thibaut, Adam, and the Medieval Readers of the *Chansonnier de Noailles* (T-*trouv*.)." In *Musical Culture in the World of Adam de la Halle,* edited by Jennifer Saltzstein, 121–50. Leiden and Boston, MA: Brill, 2019.

———. ed. *Medieval Music in Practice: Studies in Honor of Richard Crocker.* Middleton, WI: American Institute of Musicology, 2013.

Pesce, Dolores. "Beyond Glossing: The Old Made New in *Mout me fu grief/Robin m'aime/Portare.*" In *Hearing the Motet: Essays on the Motet of the Middle Ages and Renaissance,* edited by Dolores Pesce, 28–51. New York and Oxford: Oxford University Press, 1997.

———. ed. *Hearing the Motet: Essays on the Motet of the Middle Ages and Renaissance.* New York and Oxford: Oxford University Press, 1997.

Pfändtne, Karl-Georg. "Zum Enstehungsraum der Bamberger Motettenhandschrift Msc. Lit. 115 – kodikologische und kunsthistorische Argumente." *Acta musicologica* 84 (2012): 161–66.

Pfeffer, Wendy. "Complaints of Women and Complaints by Women: Can One Tell Them Apart?" In *The Court Reconvenes: Courtly Literature across the Disciplines,* edited by. Barbara K. Altmann, and Carleton W. Carroll, 125–32. International Courtly Literary Society 1998. Cambridge and Rochester, NY: D. S. Brewer, 2003.

Refrain (http://refrain.ac.uk/) prepared by Anne Ibos-Augé.

Regalado, Nancy Freeman. "Picturing the Story of Chivalry in Jacques Bretel's *Tournoi de Chauvency* (Oxford, Bodleian Library, MS Douce 308)." In *Tributes to Jonathan J. G. Alexander,* edited by S. L. Engle and G. B. Guest, 341–56. London: Harvey Miller, 2006.

Rizzuti, Alberto. "Torino 6 unica: Un'indagine preliminare sul manoscritto Varia 42/2 della Biblioteca Reale." *Studi Francesi* 190 (LXIV/1) (2020): 84–112.

Rothenberg, David J. "The Gate that Carries Christ: Wordplay and Liturgical Imagery in a Motet from ca. 1300." In *Music and Culture in the Middle Ages and Beyond: Liturgy, Sources, Symbolism,* edited by Benjamin Brand and David J. Rothenberg, 225–41. Cambridge: Cambridge University Press, 2016.

Roy, Bruno, ed. *L'Art d'amours: Traduction et commentaire de l'Ars amatoria de Ovide.* Leiden: E. J. Brill, 1974.

Saint-Cricq, Gaël. "Formes types dans le motet du xiiie siècle: Étude d'un processus répétitif." 2 vols. Ph.D. diss., University of Southampton, 2009.

———. "Introduction." In *Motets from the Chansonnier de Noailles,* edited by Gaël Saint-Cricq, with Eglal Doss-Quinby and Samuel N. Rosenberg, xv–xlii. Middleton, WI: A-R Editions, Inc., 2017.

Saltzstein, Jennifer. "Adam de la Halle's Fourteenth-Century Musical and Poetic Legacies." In *Musical Culture in the World of Adam de la Halle,* edited by Jennifer Saltzstein, 352–63. Leiden and Boston, MA: Brill, 2019.

———. "Introduction." In *Musical Culture in the World of Adam de la Halle,* edited by Jennifer Saltzstein, 1–17. Leiden and Boston, MA: Brill, 2019.

———. "Ovid and the Thirteenth-Century Motet: Quotation, Reinterpretation, and Vernacular Hermeneutics." *Musica disciplina* 58 (2013): 351–72.
———. *The Refrain and the Rise of the Vernacular in Medieval French Music and Poetry*. Gallica 30. Woodbridge, Suffolk and Rochester, NY: D. S. Brewer, 2013.
———. "Relocating the Thirteenth-Century Refrain: Intertextuality, Authority and Origins." *Journal of the Royal Musical Association* 135 (2010): 245–79.
———, ed. *Musical Culture in the World of Adam de la Halle*. Leiden and Boston, MA: Brill, 2019.
Skoda, Hannah. *Medieval Violence: Physical Brutality in Northern France 1270–1330*. Oxford: Oxford University Press, 2013.
Songs of the Women Troubadours. Edited and translated by Matilda Tomaryn Bruckner, Laurie Shepard, and Sarah White. Garland Library of Medieval Literature A, 97. New York: Garland Publishing, 1995.
Songs of the Women Trouvères. Edited, translated, and introduced by Eglal Doss-Quinby, Joan Tasker Grimbert, Wendy Pfeffer, and Elizabeth Aubrey. New Haven, CT: Yale University Press, 2001.
Spanke, Hans G., ed. *Eine altfranzösische Liedersammlung: Der anonyme Teil der Liederhandschriften K N P X*. Halle: Max Niemeyer, 1925.
———. *Raynaud's Bibliographie des altfranzösischen Liedes*. Musicologica 1. Leiden: Brill, 1955.
Steffens, Georg, ed. *Die Lieder des Troveors Perrin von Angicourt*. Halle: Max Niemeyer, 1905.
Steiner, Ruth. "Ave regina caelorum." https://www.encyclopedia.com/religion/encyclopedias-almanacs-transcripts-and-maps/ave-regina-caelorum.
Stones, Alison. "Another Note on fr. 25566 and Its Illustrations." In *Musical Culture in the World of Adam de la Halle*, edited by Jennifer Saltzstein, 77–94. Leiden and Boston, MA: Brill, 2019.
———. Appendix IV. "Illustrated Miracles de Nostre Dame Manuscripts Listed by Stylistic Attribution and Attributable Manuscripts whose MND Section is Unillustrated." In *Gautier de Coinci: Miracles, Music, and Manuscripts*, ed. Kathy M. Krause and Alison Stones. Medieval Texts and Cultures of Northern Europe 13. Turnhout: Brepols, 2006.
———. *Gothic Manuscripts 1260–1320*. 4 vols. London and Turnhout: Harvey Miller Publishers, 2013–14.
———. "The Style and Iconography of Montpellier folio 350r." In *The Montpellier Codex: The Final Fascicle*, edited by Catherine A. Bradley and Karen Desmond, 66–77. Woodbridge and Rochester NY: Boydell Press, 2018.
Symes, Carol. *A Common Stage: Theater and Public Life in Medieval Arras*. Conjunctions of Religion and Power in the Medieval Past. Ithaca, NY: Cornell University Press, 2007.
———. "The 'School of Arras' and the Career of Adam." In *Musical Culture in the World of Adam de la Halle*, edited by Jennifer Saltzstein, 21–50. Leiden and Boston, MA: Brill, 2019.

Tischler, Hans, ed. *The Earliest Motets (to circa 1270): A Complete Comparative Edition.* New Haven, CT: Yale University Press, 1982.

———. ed. *The Montpellier Codex.* Recent Researches in the Music of the Middle Ages and Early Renaissance, vols. 2–8. Madison, WI: A-R Editions, Inc., 1978–85.

van den Boogaard, Nico H. J. *Rondeaux et refrains du XIIe siècle au début du XIVe.* Paris: Klincksieck, 1969.

van der Werf, Hendrik. *Integrated Directory of Organa, Clausulae, and Motets.* Rochester, NY: Hendrik van der Werf, 1989.

Vilamo-Pentti, Eva, ed. *La Court de Paradis, poème anonyme du XIIIe siècle.* Helsinki: Société de Littérature Finnoise, 1953.

Wolinski, Mary E. "The Compilation of the Montpellier Codex." *Early Music History* 11 (1992): 263–301.

Index of Compositions

Note: Page numbers followed by "n" denote footnotes.

Amis, vostre demoree/DECANTATUR (**Mo** 6, 212) 42, 44–46, 47, 52, 65n11, 80–82, 84, 86, 117, 120–21, 123, 124

A tort sui d'amours blasmee /[IMMO] LATUS (**Mo** 6, 180) 16n5, 21–23, 61–62, 80, 82, 84, 85–86, 115, 118, 120, 123–24

Ave, virgo regia/Ave, plena gracie/ FIAT (**Ba** no. 3) 51

Biaus dous amis, quel conseil me donrés?/Grant pechlet fist cis qui m'a mariée)/VALE (**Tu**, f. 16) 17, 40–41, 62n3, 62n4, 120, 120n8, 123

Cele m'a s'amour/ALLELUIA. HODIE MARIA VIRGO CELOS ASCENDIT. GAUDETE, QUIA CUM CHRISTO REGNAT (**N(mo)**, no. 84) 88–90, 111, 124

Cest quadruble sans reison/Voz n'i dormirés ja mais/Biaus cuers renvoisiés et douz /FIAT (**Mo** 2, 30) 42, 46–52, 53, 87, 111–13, 118, 121–22, 123

Dame bele et avenant et de biau port/ Fi, mari, de vostre amour! /NUS N'IERT JA JOLIS, S'IL N'AIME (**Mo** 7, 271) 54–55, 59, 63, 69–72, 76–77, 85, 116, 118–19, 120–21

Dame, que j'aim et desir/Amors vaint tot fors cuer de felon/Au tans d'esté, que cil oisel /ET GAUDEBIT (**Mo** 2, 23) 16, 23–25, 36–38, 87, 104–10, 115, 116, 118, 121, 122, 123, 125

Dieus, je n'i os aler a ma dame parler/ Amours, qui m'aprist de ses geus/ET SUPER (**Mo** 5, 101) 93–97

Fi, mari, de vostre amour (polyphonic rondeau, Adam de la Halle) 69–72

Hier main jouer m'en alai/[IMMO] LATUS (**Mo** 6, 203) 16, 19–21, 22, 77–80, 80n42, 82, 84–85, 115, 16, 118, 120–21, 123–24

Hyer main chevauchoie/PORTARE (**Mo** 6, 233) 16, 28, 36, 37, 77n39, 87–91, 110–11, 115, 116, 117–18, 120, 121–22, 122n10, 123–24

Ja ne mi marierai /AMORIS (EM 310) 26, 62n3, 63–66, 76, 85, 115, 117–18, 120–21, 123–24

Je m'en vois, ma douce amie/Tieus a mout le cuer hardi/OMNES (**Mo** 5, 80) 93–97, 102

Je sui jonete et jolie/Hé! Dieus, je n'ai pas mari /VERITATEM (**Mo** 5, 156) 28, 29–31, 62n4, 115, 118, 120n8, 123

Li jalous par tout son fustat/Tuit cil qui sunt enamourat/VERITATEM (**Mo** 5, 169) 16, 28, 31–35, 63, 82–84, 86, 115, 118, 120–21, 123

[Nus ne se doit ...] /[Je sui en melencolie ...]/[AVE VERUM CORPUS] (**Mo** 7, 276) 16, 42–44, 52–53, 62n4, 115, 118, 120n8

Nus ne set les biens d'amors/Ja Dieus ne me doinst corage/PORTARE (**Mo** 5, 142) 23, 28, 36–38, 87, 104–109, 110, 115, 16, 118, 121–22, 122n10, 123–25

Osteis lou moi (EM 389, motet text only) 54, 58–59, 62n3, 63, 66–69, 76, 80n42, 85, 116, 117, 120–21, 123

Par un matinet l'autrier/Hé sire, que voz vantés/EIUS (**Mo** 2, 22) 111–12

Post partum virgo mansisti/Ave, regina glorie/VERITATEM (**Mo** 4, 64) 83, 83n49, 84, 118, 123

Pour quoi m'avés voz douné / DOCEBIT (**Mo** 6, 243) 26, 61, 62n4, 77n39, 115, 118, 120n8, 123

Quant la froidor trait a fin/L'autrier chevauchoie/NOSTRUM (**Mo** 5, 106) 109–10, 116

Renvoisiement irai a la bele, que j'aim tant/D'Amours sunt en grant esmai/ ET SUPER (**Mo** 5, 97) 91, 98–99, 103, 121

Si com<e> aloie jouer/Deduisant com fins amourous/PORTARE (**Mo** 5, 148) 16, 20n2, 28, 38–39, 87, 91–104, 110, 115, 16, 118–19, 121–22, 122n10, 123

S'on me regarde, s'on me regarde/ Prennés i garde, s'on me regarde/ HÉ MI ENFANT (**Mo** 8, 325) 54, 55–58, 59, 63, 72–76, 76–77, 85, 116, 118, 120–21, 123

Tant me fait a vos penser/Tout li cuers me rit de joie/OMNES (**Mo** 5, 115) 100–2

Trop sui jonette, maris (EM 415, motet text only) 59, 62n4, 120n8

Un chant renvoisie/DECANTATUR (**ArsB**, f. 14) 44, 81

General Index

Note: Page numbers followed by "n" denote footnotes.

Adam de la Halle *see* rondeau
agency 8, 9, 59, 104
Albertus Magnus 4
allegory(allegorical, allegorize) i, 2, 12, 16, 20, 20n2, 23, 25–27, 34, 34n13, 36, 44, 44n1, 46, 46n10, 52, 66, 76, 80, 81, 85, 86, 89, 100n17, 115, 124
Andreas Capellanus, *De amore* 5
Aristotle 4
Arras i, 10n33, 11n35, 45, 63, 64, 65n11, 67, 69, 72, 73, 76, 77, 80–81, 87–88, 91n7, 100, 120–21, 122n10, 123–24
Artois (Artesian) 10, 12, 29n2, 63–65, 67, 76, 77–78, 81, 82, 83, 84, 87, 90–91, 100, 102, 117–18, 120–21, 122n10, 123–25
Atchison, Mary 58n5, 66n13
Aubry, Elizabeth 84

Baldwin, John W. 2n5, 3n8, 4n10, 5
Baltzer, Rebecca 25n8, 73n32
Bec, Pierre 6, 15–16
Bleisch, Nicholas W. 64n8
Blonquist, Lawrence B. 4n12
Bradley, Catherine A. 28n1, 44–46, 48n14, 61n1, 62, 70n25, 71–72, 73n32, 80, 81n46, 81, 117n1
Brundage, James A. 10
Büttner, Fred 61n1
Buffum, Douglas Labaree 64n1
Burr, Kristin L. 64n3

Butterfield, Ardis 64n2, 64, 65n10, 67n17, 99n15

Callahan, Christopher 64n8, 67n16, 80n42, 107n27, 117n1
Cambrai 44, 81n46, 84
canonist i, 2, 4, 10, 11
canso 5–7
carole 33–34, 56–57, 63, 65, 82
Catalunya, David 118n3
chanson avec des refrains: *Chançon veul faire de moi* (Perrin d'Angicourt) 64–66, 76; *En mi mai quant s'est la saisons partie* (Guillaume le Vinier) 77–80; *Li beaus tens d'esté* (Colart le Boutellier) 100; *Penser ne doit vilanie* (Jehan Erart) 100; *Quant li douz tans rasouage* (anon.) 77–80; *Quant se resjouissent oisel* (anon. or Thibaut de Blaison) 21, 80; *Se felon et losengier* (Philippe or Jeannot Paon) 107
chanson d'ami 1, 15, 24
chanson de femme 1, 6–7, 15; *Amours me fait renvoisier et chanter* (Moniot d'Arras) 45, 47, 52, 65n11, 80–81, 121
chanson de malmariée 1, 6, 7, 15, 16n5, 47, 50, 65n11
chanson pieuse 16n5, 22, 80, 82, 85–86
Chrétien de Troyes, *Eric et Enide* and *Cligès* 5
Christ: as Bridegroom 26, 29, 34, 35n15, 36, 86 (*see also* marriage,

158 General Index

mystical); self-sacrifice 19, 20, 23, 80, 85, 86
clausula 61–62, 80, 84, 118, 120, 123
Colart le Boutellier *see chanson avec des refrains*
Conrad of Marburg 46, 52; *see also* St. Elizabeth of Hungary, beatings
contrafact 11n35, 12, 51–52, 53, 61, 112–13, 121n9
Court d'amours x, c, 63. 67, 70
La Court de Paradis xi, 33–34, 63, 82–84, 86, 100–102, 122n10
cuckold (*cous*) 8–9, 16, 32, 34, 39, 45, 58–59, 68, 114
Curran, Sean 73n32, 119

David de Dinant, *Quarternuli* 4
d'Avray, David 35n15
Dell, Helen 9–11
Dolce, Brianne 11n35
Doss-Quinby, Eglal 1n1, 58n4, 88n1, 104n25
Dronke, Peter 7n25
Duby, Georges 2n4, 3n8
Duchess de Lorraine 8

empower 24, 38, 107, 116
Everist, Mark 55n1, 69n24, 70–72, 73n35, 75n36, 83–84, 88n2, 91n7, 104n25

fabliau 3–4, 5, 10, 49
fantasy: female 1, 11, 36, 59, 117; male 11, 24, 36, 38, 107
fol(*ie*) 42–44, 52, 112
Frank, István 83n48, 83n49

Gaunt, Simon B. 5n16
gelos 7, 32; *see also* marriage, jealous husband
gender(ed) roles 17, 116; in conception (*see* marriage)
gender issues i, 12, 125
gender symmetry *see* marriage
Gennrich, Friedrich xv, 17, 104n25
Gerard of Liège *see Quinque incitamenta ad Deum amandum ardenter*
Gerbert de Montreuil *see Roman de la Violette*

grand chant courtois 2, 5, 6, 16, 40; aristocratic love 55, 85; desirable female traits 42–43, 55, 98; desirable male traits 38, 88; ennobling effects 37; idealized love 24, 37, 44, 53, 112–13, 116; male voice 2, 24, 27, 37, 42, 44, 50, 52, 54, 72, 88–89, 95–97, 98, 100–1, 104, 107, 110; rhetoric of pain 24, 37, 45, 55, 88–89; unfulfilled love (unconsummated, unrequited) 44, 55, 59, 88–89
Gratian, *Decretum* 2
Grau, Anna Kathryn 1n3, 21n5, 47, 56–57, 58n3, 65n11
Gravdal, Kathryn 49
Grimbert, Joan Tasker 6n19
Guilhem IX 7
Guillaume d'Amiens *see* rondeau
Guillaume le Vinier *see chanson avec des refrains*

Haines, John 69, 75n35
Heloise 5
Hoekstra, Gerald R. 25n8
Huot, Sylvia 20, 21, 26n10, 30–31, 32–34, 37n16, 44n1, 46n10, 50, 58n4, 66n14, 88, 100, 114

Ibos-Augé, Anne 18n9, 67n17, 69n24, 71n30, 83, 102n20
idealized love *see grand chant courtois*
intertextual(ity) i, 2, 12, 52, 58, Part II *passim*, Conclusion *passim*
irony 20, 116

Jacquemart Giélée *see Renart le nouvel*
Jean Renart *see Roman de la rose* or *Guillaume de Dole*
Jeanroy, Alfred 7, 32
Jehan Erart *see chanson avec des refrains*
Jenkins, T. Atkinson 29n2
Johnson, Susan M. 15–16, 21, 79n40

Karp, Theodore 64n6
Kenney, E.J. 5n13
kharjas 7
Klinck, Anne L. 1n2, 11n35

General Index   159

Larrington, Carolyne 2n4
L'Art d'amours xi, 4, 47–50, 53, 99, 111–12, 122n10; *see also* Ovid, *Ars amatoria*
Lorraine 8, 12, 58, 64, 66n15, 76, 77–78, 84, 117, 120–21, 123
Ludwig, Friedrich xv, 17, 71n30
Lug, Robert 67n16

Makowski, Elizabeth M. 3n7
Marie, countess of Champagne 5, 29n2
Marie de France, *Yoned* and *Guigemar* 5
marriage: abusive husband 7, 10, 117; arranged 3, 26, 30–31, 49, 58, 59, 68–69, 76, 85, 114; consummation 2; defiance(ant) wife 1, 8, 9, 21, 24, 27, 31, 37, 39, 55, 68, 80, 82, 85, 110, 114, 115; domestic violence 10; extra-marital 9, 20, 24, 39, 55; forced sexual relations 3, 8; gender roles in conception 3, 4; gender symmetry 2–5; helplessness of wife 9; jealous husband 7, 8, 16, 30, 31–34, 38–39, 41, 45–47, 50n17, 56–58, 59, 65n11, 75–76, 80–81, 86, 93, 97, 99; marital debt 2–3, 5, 8, 16, 31, 114; marital bondage (*vincula nuptualis* and *matrimonii foedera*) 4, 5; moral sense of wife 39, 59, 97; mutual consent 2–3, 4–5, 16, 114; mystical 29, 34–35, 40; self-fulfillment/satisfaction of wife 20, 23, 59, 80, 88, 107
May fests (*fêtes de mai, maieroles*) 7, 32–34, 86
Ménard, Philippe 79n41
Menuge, Noël James 3n9
Metz 58, 64, 66, 67, 80, 120
mock(ery) 9, 10, 11, 20, 43, 46, 52, 59, 114, 116–17
Moniot d'Arras *see chanson de femme*
monologue 1, 16, 40
Montpellier Codex ix, xiii, 12, 17, 48n14, 70n25, 73, 91n7, 117, 124, *et passim*
muwashshaha 7

narrator 2, 15, 16, 19–21, 36, 68–69, 76, 78–80, 82, 85, 90, 109, 114, 115–16; *see also pastourelle*, encounter frame
Newman, Barbara 81n45
Noailles chansonnier ix, x, 12, 62, 91n7, *et passim*

oral tradition 7
Ovid, *Ars amatoria* 4, 5n13, 47, 99; *see also L'Art d'amours*

Page, Christopher 33n10
parody(parodic) i, 2, 12, 16, 19–21, 23–27, 28, 31, 34, 36, 37, 39, 40, 41, 43–44, 46, 49n16, 52, 55, 59, 66, 72, 76–77, 80, 84, 85–86, 87–89, 104, 107, 111, 113, 115, 116, 122, 124
pastourelle avec des refrains: *En une praele* (anon.) 67–68
pastourelle: encounter frame 2, 15–16, 19, 21, 24, 36, 38, 68, 78, 79, 85, 90, 115–16; shepherdess 2, 15–16, 21, 36, 50, 75, 77, 85, 90, 109, 110, 115–17
patriarchal society 2
Peraino, Judith A. 87n1
Perrin d'Angicourt *see chanson avec des refrains*
Pesce, Dolores 35n14, 121n9
Peter Lombard, *Sententiae* 2
Pfändtne, Karl-Georg 51n18, 119n6
Philippe or Jeannot Paon *see chanson avec des refrains*
Picardy 10n33, 77–78, 81
Picardy-Artois 64–65, 67, 76, 93, 100, 107, 120, 122n10
play 2, 23, 36, 40, 41, 44, 52, 76, 80, 85, 109, 114–17, 124; intergeneric 12, 16, 21, 61, 77, 85, 89, 109, 115–16, 123, 125; *see also* allegory; parody
Pope Alexander III 2
Psalm 44 29, 32, 34, 41; *Alleluia. Veni electa mea* 34, 88; Gradual *Propter veritatem* 29, 30, 34 (*see also* tenor, *VERITATEM*); mystical marriage 29, 34–35, 40; wedding song 29

Psalm 72, divine justice 50–51, 53; *see also* tenor, *FIAT*

Quinque incitamenta ad Deum amandum ardenter (Gerard of Liège) xi, 81n45

refrain: vdB 189 21–22, 80; vdB 217 48–50, 111–12; vdB 286 23; vdB 532 38–39, 91–97, 102, 110; vdB 587 23, 36–37, 105–7, 110; vdB 664 24, 105, 109–10; vdB 746 55, 69–72; vdB 748 24–25, 109; vdB 750 38, 91–93, 97–99, 102–3, 110, 121; vdB 900 23, 36, 104, 105, 107–8, 110, 122n10; vdB 971 23; vdB 1006 26, 63–66, 76; vdB 1374 26, 63; vdB 1407 54, 69–72; vdB 1463 58, 67–69, 76; vdB 1489 38–39, 91–93, 98–99, 102; vdB 1531 56–58, 73–76; vdB 1540 51–52, 11–13, 122; vdB 1555 45, 65n11, 80–82; vdB 1691 36, 87–91, 111, 121; vdB 1781 38, 91–93, 99–102, 110; vdB 1822 32–33, 82; vdB 1842 55, 69, 71–72; vdB 1856 19–20, 77–80; vdB 1867 47–48, 49–50, 111–12

Regalado, Nancy Freeman 66n15
register 6, 15
religious profession 26, 115
Renart le Nouvel (Jacquemart Giélée) x, 63, 67, 69, 73–75
Rizzuti, Alberto 41n17
roman à chansons 64
Roman de la rose or *Guillaume de Dole* (Jean Renart) 5, 64, 65n10, 65n11, 66, 67n17
Roman de la Violette (Gerbert de Montreuil) x, 50n17, 63–66, 76
rondeau: *Fi, mari, de vostre amour* (Adam de la Halle) 54, 69–72, 76–77, 85; *HÉ MI ENFANT 55; Nus n'iert ja jolis* (anon.) 54, 69–72; *Prendés i garde, s'on mi regarde* (attrib. Guillaume d'Amiens) 73–76
Rosenberg, Samuel N. 22n6, 58n4
Roy, Bruno 4n12

Saint-Cricq, Gaël 62, 87n1, 88, 90–91, 117n1

St. Elizabeth of Hungary: beatings 45–46, 52, 81–82, 86; *see also* marriage, abusive husband; *DECANTATUR* tenor 44, 52, 77, 81n46, 84
Saltzstein, Jennifer xv, 4n12, 12n36, 52, 64n1, 69n23, 96, 99n15
self-sacrifice: of Christ (*see* Christ, self-sacrifice); of Mary (*see* Virgin Mary, selfless); *see also* marriage, self-fulfillment
Skoda, Hannah 10–11
Spanke, Hans G. 18n9, 64n7
Steffens, Georg 65n9
Steiner, Ruth 41n18
Stones, Alison 73, 81n44, 81
Symes, Carol 69n21

tenor: *AMORIS* (Pentecost) 25–27, 63, 66, 115; *AVE VERUM CORPUS* (Eucharistic chant) 42–44; *DECANTATUR* (*see* St. Elizabeth of Hungary); *DOCEBIT* (Pentecost) 25–27, 115; *ET GAUDEBIT* (Ascension) 23, 25, 37, 87, 104, 122; *FIAT* (Holy Trinity) 46–47, 50–52, 87, 111, 113, 121; *HÉ MI ENFANT* 55, 72; *IMMOLATUS* (Easter) 19–22, 26, 77, 80, 85, 115; *NUS N'IERT JA JOLIS, S'IL N' AIME* 54, 69–72; *PORTARE* (Assumption) 28, 35–40, 87–111, 113, 115, 121–22, 124; *VERITATEM* (Assumption) 28, 29–32, 34, 39–40, 82–83, 86, 115, 123; *VALE* 40–41
Thibaut de Blaison *see* chanson avec des refrains
Thomas Aquinas 4
Tischler, Hans xv, 17, 22n6, 104n25
Tournoi de Chauvency 66, 67n17
trobaritz 6n17

van den Boogaard, Nico H. J. xv, 17–18; *see also* refrain, vdB numbers
van der Werf, Hendrik 17n8, 47n11
vil[l]ain (villain) 30, 31, 37, 41, 47–49, 55, 58, 68, 71, 79, 105, 112
Vilamo-Pentti, Eva 33n7

Virgin Mary: as Bride of Christ 13, 28, 29, 35, 37, 39, 40, 41, 86, 89, 104, 111, 115, 122 (*see also* marriage, mystical); devotion to Christ 28, 35, 40, 115; as intercessor 28, 41; as Queen of Heaven 28, 33, 41, 63, 82; selfless 28, 31, 40, 89, 115, 122

Voice: female 1, 2, 6, 7, 15–16, 20, 21, 29, 31, 36, 37, 39, 40, 44–45, 47, 49, 52, 54, 56, 69, 75, 77, 85, 86, 96, 107, 109, 110, 115, 116; intertextual switch of speaker's gender 12, 61, 77, 98, 104, 110, 116; male (*see grand chant courtois*); male-female dialogue 2, 48–50, 88, 113; married man expressing discontent 16, 43–44, 52, 115; third-person 16, 31, 86

Wagner, Peter 41

Wolinski, Mary E. 48n14

For Product Safety Concerns and Information please contact our EU representative GPSR@taylorandfrancis.com
Taylor & Francis Verlag GmbH, Kaufingerstraße 24, 80331 München, Germany

www.ingramcontent.com/pod-product-compliance
Lightning Source LLC
Chambersburg PA
CBHW051746230426
43670CB00012B/2180